How To Do A
Section 1031
Like Kind
Exchange

Simultaneous, Delayed, Reverse, Construction

Michael Lantrip
Attorney at Law

Free updates at
www.S1031Exchange.com

THE AUTHOR

Michael Lantrip, Attorney at Law, is licensed to practice law in Texas, North Carolina, Virginia, and the District of Columbia.

Formerly a Tax Examiner for the Internal Revenue Service, and Tax Accountant for a Big 8 Accounting Firm, he has also worked as a Newspaper Reporter, Radio News Director, Television Executive News Producer, and Military Intelligence Analyst.

He is admitted to practice in all Courts in Texas, North Carolina, Virginia, and the District of Columbia, as well as the U.S. Tax Court, the U.S. Federal District Court, and the D.C. Court of Appeals.

He practices in the fields of Business Law, Real Estate Law, U.S. Tax Law, and International Business and Tax Law.

He has a B.B.A. in Finance from the University of Houston School of Business, and a Juris Doctor in Law from the University of Texas Law School.

In addition to 32 years of practicing law, he built and operated his own Title Insurance Company, and has been an Approved Title Attorney for seven national Title Insurance Underwriters.

He has handled over two thousand real estate transactions.

This book is the composite of all of that experience.

You can find more information at www.MichaelLantrip.com.

FREE UPDATES!

Tax Law changes almost daily. Therefore, when you are reading anything about the tax laws, you should always note the publication date.

The content that you are finding on the web might be current, but more likely it was taken from somewhere else, was created at an earlier date, and therefore is probably not current. Even a print publication will not be current. It often reflects the situation as it existed at the time the research was done by the writer, which could be as long as one year before.

This publication, How To Do A Section 1031 Like Kind Exchange, both digital and print, is current as of the date of publication, and it will be constantly updated, so it will always be current.

And you don't have to do a thing. I'll notify you of the updates!

Following the initial 2017 publication, the website S1031Exchange.com will publish all changes and updates in the book's content as they occur, and will continue to do so until the updated edition is produced in 2019. The updates will be available to everyone visiting the site, but buyers of the book will receive email notification and access to a download page, along with a complete explanation of the meaning of the update.

For signup and complete details, visit S1031Exchange.com.

If you have the print book, the site will contain corrected pages for you to print and insert in the book.

If you have the eBook, it will be constantly updated with the retailers, so that new customers will always receive the newest version.

For existing customers, only iBooks will notify you that there is an updated version, and you can download it for free, and it automatically replaces the older copy in your library.

If you are a Smashwords customer, you can always re-download the newest version, after I have notified you of the changes.

Kindle will provide free updates, but you must be careful. First, go to your "Manage Your Content and Devices" page, make sure to turn on your Annotations Backup feature, and then turn on "Automatic Book Update."

For Barnes & Noble customers who have already downloaded the eBook to their Nook, it will not be replaced automatically, but if you archive and re-download the book, you will get the updated file free. However, Nook does not notify the customer of the available update, and does not share customer information with anyone, including the author, so you must go to S1031Exchange.com to sign up for the notifications so that I can let you know, and so that I can explain the changes to you.

And finally, KOBO does not allow file updates.

I have made every effort that I can think of to make sure that this book will be fresh and new every time you pick it up to use it.

Thank you for being a reader.

INTRODUCTION

Now, let's get to the subject matter of the book. This is really good stuff.

Section 1031 of the Internal Revenue Code makes it possible for you to start with a real estate investment of, say $40,000, and turn that into income property worth as much as $10,000,000 in only 30 years, through a series of sales and purchases in which you defer all taxes on your profits with each transaction. You can then eliminate most, or all, of the deferred tax liability with careful planning.

This book is not about how to get rich quickly. It is more about how to get very rich, slowly and safely.

This book is not intended to be legal advice nor financial advice about what you should do. It is an explanation of "How To Do A Section 1031 Like Kind Exchange" if you decide for yourself to include this technique in your tax and estate planning. You should always get professional advice concerning your specific circumstances before you make any decision.

Now, let's talk about Section 1031.

Section 1031 is not a "loophole" (defined as "an ambiguity or inadequacy in the law or a set of rules; synonym: means of evasion"), like the hucksters and promoters would have you believe, as though the IRS didn't know what they were doing, and just screwed up, and now they can't fix it. That didn't happen.

Section 1031 reflects long-standing government policy with a national purpose and intent. And it is here for every American citizen who wants to use it.

Also, a Section 1031 Exchange is not "tax-free" and it is not "tax-exempt" as it is sometimes characterized. It is "tax-deferred," which means that you will not be taxed on the profit from the sale of your investment or business property at the time of sale, if you agree to re-invest those proceeds into other "like kind" property (which you were probably planning to do anyway). The arrangement benefits you because you don't have to pay the taxes on your profits, and the arrangement benefits the government because the economy is stimulated with investments which produce other sources of taxation. The government knows that eventually the taxes will be paid, the taxes are just being deferred to a later time.

However, there are a number of ways that, by following all of the rules, the deferred taxes don't ever actually become due, and these methods are not challenged by the IRS. In fact, the procedure for doing so is laid out in detail by the IRS in the Treasury Regulations.

You should read this book from the beginning. I will use real-life scenarios, real-life characters, and real-life transactions to explain each step of the process. Each step will build on the previous step. And I will use the same Example throughout, only making small changes for discussion purposes. The earlier Examples will be very simplified, and only the latter ones will contain the factors that you are likely to encounter in your personal situation.

It will be a journey of knowledge and understanding, building a strong foundation for investment decision-making along the way. Please be patient.

Now, let's save some taxes!

Publisher: ANDERSON LOGAN, LLC

First Edition
Version 1.0

ISBN 978-1-945627-00-2

DISCLAIMER

Although I am a lawyer, I am not your lawyer. Reading this book does not create an attorney-client relationship between us. This book should not be used as a substitute for the advice of a competent attorney admitted or authorized to practice law in your jurisdiction.

Contents

FREE MONEY TIMES FIVE, THEN TIMES THIRTY

OVERVIEW

In order to give you an understanding of the tremendous power available to a taxpayer using the Section 1031 Like Kind Exchange provisions when selling property, I have presented a simplified overview of a real transaction.

HOW IT WORKS

The first thing for you to understand about deferring payment of the tax on your capital gains (your profit) is this: when you do, the money you are keeping, and then using to invest in new projects, is money that, in effect, is not really yours.

And it's not borrowed money, either. It's better than borrowed money because you don't have to pay interest on it or make monthly payments.

Really, it is money that you will eventually owe to the IRS, but that you don't have to pay until you're ready, and you might never have to pay it.

In other words, you are using the IRS's money to invest in real estate. And they know it, they are fine with it, and they want you to do it. That's why Section 1031 exists.

And it gets even better!

You are also using the IRS's money as the basis for borrowing four times that amount, ending up with an investment nest egg made up entirely of other people's money, the IRS's 20% and the bank's 80%, but managed by you and used to build your own real estate portfolio.

Think about that!

This happens because when the typical bank makes a real estate investment loan, they require the borrower to provide a down payment of 20%, and then they loan the other 80%. (You might borrow your funds somewhere other than a bank, and you might actually get 90% or 100% financing if you have a strong enough Financial Statement, or relationship with the lender, but we'll work here with an 80% bank loan because that is the norm. Also, we are assuming that you are a bona fide real estate investor with a history, not someone with no regular income and no assets.)

In our example, imagine that you sell a business or investment asset, such as a Duplex, and make a profit of, say $200,000. You will incur a capital gains tax liability of $40,000 which you will send to the IRS. The highest capital gain tax rate is 20%, so .20 X $200,000 = $40,000. But then, you don't pay that. You defer payment of the capital gains taxes by purchasing a replacement property, and engaging in a Section 1031 Like Kind Exchange. In other words, you use your net sales proceeds to buy another business or investment asset of equal or greater value. That means that you don't have to pay the $40,000 in capital gains tax to the IRS. You keep the $40,000. And that $40,000 tax bill disappears into the Replacement Property, and stays there until you sell the Replacement Property. And when you do eventually sell it, you can delay the existing tax liability again on this current transaction, and also on that second transaction, by doing another Section 1031 Exchange.

(Your federal tax bill would actually be about $55,000 instead of $40,000 but we will explain all of that later, and for now just work with the $40,000 figure).

It's true, you can't use any of the money that represents your capital gains for anything you want, it must all be rolled over into the Replacement Property along with all of your net sales proceeds (but, see Chapter 8 on how you can actually get this money out tax-free and use it).

Let's assume that you walk away from the closing table with $200,000 net sales proceeds, the same amount as your capital gains. For purposes of illustration, so that we can track what happens to the $40,000 that you don't send to the IRS, let's assume that you buy two Replacement Properties with all of your net sales proceeds instead of buying just one, which you are allowed to do. You use $160,000 of your $200,000 profit, or capital gains, get an 80% bank loan for $640,000 and purchase one property for $800,000. Now you take the remaining $40,000 that you were going to pay to the IRS and use it as your 20% down payment, get a bank loan for $160,000, and have a total of $200,000 to buy another piece of income property.

This is why I refer to it as "Free Money Times Five." Your $40,000 of free money ends up being $200,000.

This is $200,000 that you would not otherwise have had access to, if you had not deferred the capital gains taxes on the profit from the sale, because the $40,000 you are using as a down payment would have gone to the IRS, and it would be gone forever.

Now let's look at the result of just the $40,000 investment. Even if you only hold the investment for ten years, it is amazing what happens.

Assume that you use this $200,000 in funds to buy an income property that will cash flow, and pay all of your expenses, including property taxes and principal and interest on the note. This should be your strategy in any investment.

Also assume a conservative 6.0% annual appreciation in value for the property, although the real figure, based on historical data, on average, is actually 6.7% annually.

In ten years, the property will increase in value from $200,000 to $358,170.

Year 1	200,000 x 1.06	212,000
Year 2	212,000 x 1.06	224,720
Year 3	224,720 x 1.06	238,203
Year 4	238,203 x 1.06	252,495
Year 5	252,495 x 1.06	267,645
Year 6	267,645 x 1.06	283,704
Year 7	283,704 x 1.06	300,726
Year 8	300,726 x 1.06	318,770
Year 9	318,770 x 1.06	337,896
Year 10	337,896 x 1.06	358,170

This is the same as compound interest. It is the original amount multiplied by 1.06 to the tenth power (1.06 x 1.06 x 1.06, etc.), which is $200,000 times 1.79084769651.

But your equity of $40,000 has increased by 600%!

In ten years, the $160,000 bank note, using 5% interest rate for a 25-year note, will be paid down to about $120,000. Remember, the rental income is paying the interest and principal on the note.

Your $40,000 equity in the property has now become $238,170 equity ($358,170 current value - $120,000 note payoff).

Your $40,000 investment has multiplied 6 times to $238,170 and it wasn't even your $40,000.

If you cash out at this point:

Sales Proceeds	$358,170
Less: Note Payoff	(120,000)
Net Sales Proceeds	$238,170
Capital Gains (20% x 158,170)	(31,634)
Depreciation Recapture (25% x 65,400)	(16,350)
Payment of part of deferred tax *	(8,000)
Cash to Seller - After Tax	$182,186

*this is the portion of the deferred tax on the $200,000 profit that would be assigned to the $40,000 used to purchase this property.

But, if you decide to sell this property instead of cashing out, and defer taxes by engaging in another Section 1031 Like Kind Exchange, you would again transfer your capital gains, your basis, and your depreciation into the new Replacement Property.

Then you would have $238,170 to use as a down payment, qualifying you for a bank loan of $952,680 and you would be able to purchase a new property in the price range of $1,190,850.

You could be looking at a smaller apartment building, or a couple of Fourplexes, or maybe four Duplexes. You could even consider a small strip shopping mall.

Remember, you are in the position of owning about $1,200,000 of income property after ten years because you invested the $40,000 of capital gains taxes from the first transaction and $48,000 from this second transaction instead of sending it to the IRS.

The $40,000 that you held back from the IRS has now become $1,200,000 worth of income property, an increase of 30 times, in just ten years.

And, again, it wasn't even your money!

Think what the numbers are for the other $160,000 that you reinvested. Assuming the same 1.79084769651 increase in value, the $800,000 property has a Fair Market Value of $1,432,678 and a paid-down note balance of $600,000. Sale of this property would result in $832,678 in net sales proceeds, which would allow you to purchase a new 1031 Exchange property for $4,163,390. After ten years, you are holding title to $5,363,390 in income property.

And this is only doing three 1031 Exchanges in ten years.

And remember, this is a simple example, only using the 20% capital gains tax that is deferred. A Section 1031 Exchange also defers tax of up to 39.6% on recapture of the depreciation on the furnishings, 25% tax on recapture of depreciation on the buildings, and 3.8% investment (ObamaCare) tax. I'll show you how to do these later. It also doesn't include the state and municipal income taxes, which can go up to another 10%.

You might be hearing people say, "Oh, nobody does that, spend your time doing more deals." Well, there were more than 220,000 taxpayers using the 1031 Exchange to defer taxes on $33,782,046,000 of capital gains in 2010, the latest data available. That's 33 Billion, 782 Million, 46 Thousand, Dollars, of capital gains. So, somebody is doing it.

This is the world of the Section 1031 Like Kind Exchange, and it is where the serious real estate investors operate.

Welcome.

Remember to register for free updates at:
www.S1031Exchange.com

You will also find expanded articles on all aspects of Section 1031 Like Kind Exchanges, and articles on related subjects like Partnerships, LLCs, Corporations, and Joint Ventures.

Chapter 1

PLAYERS AND TERMS

I'm always excited when I embark on the learning process, as you are now doing, but I confess that sometimes I struggle at the beginning.

For me, the usual situation is that I'm given a lot of information and rules to remember, without being able to relate that information to anything that I already know, or anything that I've experienced, or anything that I plan to do. And then, toward the end of the process, I'm given some examples that are supposed to explain the rules and information.

That just doesn't work for me. By the time we get to the examples, I'm not sure I remember the rules because I couldn't relate them to anything. I'm uncomfortable.

I always end up re-writing my notes to move the examples to the beginning. Then I go through the examples and explain to myself why these things are happening the way that they are, by looking at the information and rules, and inserting them into the examples. Then it all makes sense.

I look at the facts first, and then I look at the law.

This is also the way that I've always provided legal and tax counseling throughout my career. You tell me the facts of your situation, and we start there. Then we determine what the questions are. And finally, we discuss the rules and apply them to the facts in order to reach an understanding of exactly what has happened, or might happen, and why. Then we can make the correct decisions.

I would like to do that here.

I will start by giving you the basic players in all of the scenarios.

I will also give you the terms that will be used consistently throughout the book to explain the concepts.

Then I will use Examples to show how the rules would be applied under every conceivable circumstance.

I think you'll like this process.

EXCHANGOR

This is the main character. This is you. You own the investment or business property which has appreciated in value, and which you want to sell without paying taxes on the profit, by qualifying to do a Section 1031 Like Kind Exchange. You will be selling property and then buying property, therefore you are called the Exchangor instead of the Buyer or Seller.

In our examples, you will be Alan Adams and your wife is Ann.

The Exchangor can also be a Corporation, Partnership, LLC, or any business entity. There are other special rules that apply to real estate investors, which we will discuss later.

RELINQUISHED PROPERTY

This is the property which you, the Exchangor, want to sell without paying taxes on the capital gains. It can be either business property or investment property, or both. It can be either real property or personal property, or both, but we will deal primarily with real property, with reference to personal property when it is appropriate to the explanation. But in exchanging properties, you must always exchange real property for real property, and exchange personal property for personal property. You cannot exchange real property for personal property, nor vice versa.

And the property that you are selling must be property that you have held for investment or for business purposes, and it must have been held for at least one year and one day.

In our first example, the Relinquished Property will be a Duplex, which you, the Exchangor, have owned for 10 years.

REPLACEMENT PROPERTY

This is the property that you, the Exchangor, intend to purchase to replace the Relinquished Property so that you can qualify for a Section 1031 Like Kind Exchange and not pay taxes on your capital gains. It can be either business property or investment property, or both. It can be either real property or personal property, or both, but we will deal primarily with real property, with reference to personal property when it is appropriate to the explanation. But you must exchange real property for real property, and exchange personal property for personal property. You cannot exchange real property for personal property, nor vice versa.

I know that I just told you that. But I repeated it because Replacement Property is different from Relinquished Property.

Replacement Property must be the type of property that can be held for investment or for business purposes by you. It doesn't matter what the current owner is doing with it.

In our first example, the Replacement Property will be a Fourplex.

But the Replacement Property can be a single property, or multiple properties.

And the Exchangor must take title to the Replacement Property in the same name that the Relinquished Property was held.

BUYER

This is the person who will buy the Relinquished Property from you, the Exchangor. He could be anybody, he has nothing to do with determining whether the Exchangor will be able to qualify to engage in a 1031 Exchange. It doesn't matter what the Buyer does with the property after he buys it from you. All he has to do is bring the money. The only exception to this rule is if he is a "Related Person," which we will discuss later.

In our first example, the Buyer of the Duplex, the Relinquished Property, will be Bob Baker.

SELLER

This is not you. Remember, you are the Exchangor. This is the person who owns the Replacement Property and will sell it to you. He is the "SELLER" of the Replacement Property. He, like the

BUYER (of the Relinquished Property), could also be anybody, except a Related Person, as long as he has the appropriate piece of property for you to buy. He will have nothing to do with determining whether the Exchangor can qualify for a 1031 Exchange, but he must be told that the transaction that he is entering into involves a Section 1031 Like Kind Exchange for the Exchangor. If the Replacement Property is comprised of multiple properties, there might be more than one Seller.

In our example the Seller of the Replacement Property is Carl Carter.

So, to recap, Adams sells to Baker, and buys from Carter.

The Exchangor sells the Relinquished Property to the Buyer, and purchases the Replacement Property from the Seller.

QUALIFIED INTERMEDIARY

This is the independent third party that will stand between the Exchangor and all of the parties- Buyer, Seller, Title Company, Realtor, Contractor, Attorney, Bank- anybody who becomes involved in the transaction. His purpose is to handle the money so that you, the Exchangor, never touch it or have any control over it. The rule is that if you, the Exchangor, touch or control the money from the sale of the Relinquished Property, you are disqualified from engaging in a Section 1031 Exchange. The Qualified Intermediary is paid by the Exchangor to make sure that everything is done in accordance with the rules of Section 1031, and then the Qualified Intermediary provides written proof of how it was done.

In all of our examples where a Qualified Intermediary is involved, it will be referred to as QI.

TITLE COMPANY

Real estate transactions are handled differently in different parts of the country.

In some states, an Escrow Company handles everything.

In some states, only attorneys are authorized to handle closings.

And in some states, the state has licensed a Title Company to handle real estate closings and insure title to the property.

You will know what the situation is in your state, but throughout this book I will use the Title Company reference because it is the most straightforward process.

PURCHASE PRICE

This is not the price of the new property you are buying. This is the price that you, the Exchangor, originally paid for the property that you are now selling, and which is becoming the Relinquished Property. It is the starting point of everything. It is used to determine the Basis of the property, and the Basis will determine the Capital Gains, which will determine everything else. I will explain this more in Chapter Three, but remember for now that the Purchase Price is the price that the Exchangor paid for the property that he now owns, the property that will become the Relinquished Property.

In our first example the Purchase Price that Adams paid for the property he is relinquishing, the Duplex, was $200,000.

SALES PRICE

This is the price for which the Exchangor is selling his Relinquished Property.

In our first example the Sales Price will be $400,000.

For Alan Adams, his Purchase Price was $200,000 and his Sales Price will be $400,000. These two prices refer to his Relinquished Property.

REPLACEMENT PROPERTY PRICE

This is the price of the property that will be purchased to complete the transaction, the Replacement Property. The price must be at least equal to, or greater than, the Sales Price, the price that the Relinquished Property is being sold for.

In the first example in which we deal with Replacement Property, the Replacement Property Price will be $700,000.

EXCHANGE DATE

There are two critical time limits that must be met in the 1031 Exchange process, and both of them start running on the Exchange Date. The Exchange Date is the date on which the Exchangor transfers the Relinquished Property to the Buyer.

In the examples that follow, we will use an exchange date of January 1, 2017, so that it will be easier to compute the running of the time periods.

THOSE ARE THE PLAYERS AND TERMS THAT WE WILL BE USING THROUGHOUT THE BOOK. IF YOU CAN UNDERSTAND THOSE, AND YOU CERTAINLY WILL UNDERSTAND THEM AFTER WE HAVE RUN THROUGH A FEW EXAMPLES, YOU CAN UNDERSTAND THE CONCEPT OF A SECTION 1031 LIKE KIND EXCHANGE AND HOW TO ANALYZE YOUR OWN SITUATION.

NOW, LET'S GET ON TO OUR FIRST TRANSACTION.

Chapter 2

SALE WITHOUT EXCHANGE

EXAMPLE #1 - BASIC TRANSACTION

Understanding what a sale looks like without a Like Kind Exchange will help to understand the 1031 Exchange process. Even if you already understand the process, you should read this part to become familiar with the Players and the Terms that will be used throughout the book.

We will start with simplified examples and build on them until you understand everything you need to know.

We will start with five Examples.

Remember that we are only dealing with Federal taxation here because all states have their own tax code, and some municipalities also have income taxing power, so there will probably also be state taxes, and possibly municipal taxes, due wherever you live, and, combined, they could go as high as 10%. But almost all states and localities follow the IRS Section 1031 Exchange rules, although some will add their own rules on top of that. We are also not dealing with the additional 3.8% medicare tax that is being called an investment tax. The total could be another 10-15% in addition to the federal tax, which is even more reason for you to do a Section 1031 Exchange.

EXAMPLE #1

This is the scenario that will be used throughout the book, so get familiar with it.

Alan Adams bought a Duplex ten years ago for $200,000 cash. He allocated $180,000 to the value of the building, the Duplex, and $20,000 to the value of the land where the building was located. He has rented out both sides of the Duplex. He has done necessary maintenance, but has not added to the units. He has claimed $65,400 of straight-line depreciation allowance on his tax returns. (Residential Real Estate has a depreciable life of 27.5 years. For a refresher on DEPRECIATION, see Chapter 9.)

Now he has an offer of $400,000 cash from a Buyer.

If he does this deal, he will have the following questions:

1.) Is this a taxable transaction?

2.) If so, what type of tax are we talking about?

3.) How much is the tax?

4.) What other factors besides the tax must he consider?

5.) What are the bottom line numbers for this transaction?

TAXABLE TRANSACTIONS

The IRS considers everything you own to be a capital asset.

When you sell a capital asset, you will either have a profit or a loss. That makes it a taxable transaction. If you make a profit, you will have a tax liability. If you have a loss, you will not have a tax liability, and might be able to deduct the loss from other taxable income, thereby lowering the taxes owed on the other taxable income.

You are required to report the transaction on your annual income tax return and pay the tax due.

Most sales will be reported on Form 8949, Sales and Other Dispositions of Capital Assets, where additional information is also entered, computations take place, and the bottom line number is eventually carried to Schedule D, Capital Gains and Losses, along with other numbers from other forms. The profits and losses are balanced against each other, and the bottom line number on Schedule D is then carried to the first page of your Form 1040 and is reported as part of your income.

Don't be put off by this explanation. This procedure is complex, and moderately complicated, but it is a piece of cake for an experienced tax accountant or tax attorney, and even you can learn the basics that you need to know. After all, these are the same numbers you are using to analyze your investments.

If you want to become more of an expert, there are a few decent books on the subject, but the best source of information is from the IRS website, irs.gov, and it is the Instructions for the form, Schedule D.

For now, and for all of our future examples, all we need to understand is that yes, this is a taxable transaction.

Now, let's find out which type of tax it is.

WHICH TYPE OF TAX

There are many different types of taxes. The two that we are concerned about are income taxes and capital gains taxes. As you've already learned, the type of tax we are dealing with here is capital gains taxes.

Now, within the capital gains tax, there are also two tax brackets, and they are based on how long you held the capital asset before selling.

* Short-term: you held the capital asset for one year or less.

* Long-term: you held the capital asset for more than one year.

Since Alan Adams has owned his Duplex for ten years, if he sells it, he will pay long-term capital gains tax.

We will not be dealing with short-term capital gains.

Now, let's look at how the tax will be computed.

HOW MUCH IS THE TAX

Short-term capital gains is taxed at the same tax rate as your ordinary income, things like your wages, etc. It depends on your individual tax bracket.

Long-term capital gains are taxed at different rates for each taxpayer, depending on many factors, which we cannot know for this discussion because we do not have the annual Income Statement and Balance Sheet of Adams.

Therefore, we will use a capital gains tax rate of 20% for our discussion, and you can adjust that to fit your category.

Appendix A has information about individual tax rates.

See Appendix B for information about capital gains tax rates.

Now, let's look at Depreciation, the only other factor to be considered before we do the bottom line on this transaction.

DEPRECIATION

When a taxpayer buys an investment property such as a Duplex, the money he pays is not an expense that can be deducted from the gross income from the property before the taxable income amount is determined.

Even if the taxpayer borrowed all of the money to buy the Duplex, the monthly principal payments on the note cannot be deducted, only the interest paid on the loan, because interest is a deductible business expense.

The way that the IRS makes this unfair situation into a fair situation, and encourages investors to put their money into such projects, is through Depreciation Allowance.

It is not an actual out-of-pocket expense, but the taxpayer can deduct it like other business expenses as though it were actually paid, because it is an "expense allocation."

Adams paid $200,000 for the Duplex, but part of that price was for the land, and land cannot be depreciated, only the building that is on the land. The theory behind this is that land is not "used up" in the process of producing income, like the building is. Adams allocated $20,000 value to the land and $180,000 value to the building. That means that the $180,000 that Adams allocated to the Duplex can be deducted in equal amounts each month until he deducts the entire amount. The period of time over which the property is depreciated is 27.5 years because it is Residential Rental Income Property. This results in a yearly Depreciation Allowance of $6,540, or a monthly expense allocation of $545.

Adams has owned the property for 10 years, so the total amount of Depreciation he has claimed comes to $65,400.

A full explanation of Depreciation is contained in Chapter 9, but you will learn what you need to know as we go along.

Now, we are ready to run the numbers on our first example.

RESULTS #1

Alan Adams bought a Duplex ten years ago for $200,000 cash and he has made no capital improvements. He has claimed $65,400 in depreciation. He sells the Duplex to Bob Baker for $400,000 cash.

STEPS FOR COMPUTING HIS TAX LIABILITY:

1.) Determine his "Basis" in the property.

"Basis" is the amount that he paid for the property plus any capital improvements, and minus any depreciation taken. He paid $200,000 for the property, and made no capital improvements, and deducted $65,400 depreciation. Therefore, his depreciated basis in the property is $134,600.

2.) Determine his Sales Price.

The actual number we will use in later Examples will not be the total Sales Price, but the "Net Sale Proceeds," which is the Sales Price of $400,000 less any expenses of the sale such as commission, document preparation, closing fees, title policy premiums, etc. But for purposes of illustration here we are using the round number of $400,000. We will "get more real" as we understand the basics.

3.) Determine his capital gains amount.

Capital Gains is defined as the difference between his basis in the property and what he sold the property for; in other words, the difference between $134,600 and $400,000. So, his capital gains amount is $265,400.

4.) Determine his capital gains tax bracket.
We are assuming a rate of 20%.

5.) Determine his capital gains tax liability.
If you thought this was too simple, you were right. So this part is for you.

The entire $265,400 capital gains is not capital gains for tax purposes, even though it is capital gains for IRS "definition" purposes. This will make sense in a minute.

The actual capital gains is the difference between what Adams paid for the property and what he sold it for. In other words, $200,000 (400,000 minus 200,000).

But we computed his capital gains as $265,400. So, what's the other $65,400 of his "definition" capital gains? Is it just coincidental that the number is the same as the amount of depreciation?

You're right. The other $65,400 represents the depreciation that he took on the Duplex, which lowered his Basis in the property from $200,000 to $134,600 and thereby increased his capital gains by the same amount.

So, Adams will be taxed at 20% on the $200,000 of profit, but for the $65,400 he will be required to do what is called "recapture of depreciation" and as long as the depreciation was taken equally over the life of the asset, that is, it is straight-line depreciation, the depreciation amount is taxed at a maximum tax rate of 25%. If Adams were in the 10% income tax bracket or the 15% income tax bracket, it would be taxed at 15% instead of 25%, but he is in the top marginal tax bracket of 39.6% (plus 3.8% ObamaCare tax, but we will be using just the 39.6%), so Adams will pay 25% tax on his "depreciation recapture" of the $65,400.

To sum it all up, Adams will pay 20% tax on $200,000 of true capital gains ($40,000) and 25% on the remaining $65,400 of depreciation recapture ($16,350).

So the total tax on his capital gains is $56,350 (40,000 plus 16,350).

In the next Example, we'll change some of the factors and see how they change the outcome.

Remember, we are still dealing with sales that do not involve using the provisions of Section 1031 Like Kind Exchange. We are just selling the asset and paying the taxes so that we can understand later what we are saving by doing a Section 1031 Exchange.

EXAMPLE #2 - WITH MORTGAGE

Same as Example #1, except that instead of Adams using his savings of $200,000 when he bought the Duplex ten years ago, he only used $50,000 from his own money, and got a bank loan for $150,000. The balance on that loan is now $130,000 and will be paid off from the Sales Proceeds of $400,000.

How does this change his tax liability?

RESULTS #2

This changes absolute nothing (except the amount of his "net sales proceeds" which he will be required to reinvest in his Replacement Property, which we will discuss later.)

But for purposes of computing his capital gains, it does not matter where Adams got the money that he used to purchase his Relinquished Property, whether from his savings account, or borrowed from the bank, or from his mother. He paid $200,000 for the property.

And it does not matter what deductions were made from the money that Adams received from the sale of the property, paid off a bank loan, or went on a cruise. He still received $400,000 for the property in our Example.

So his capital gains is still $265,400.

EXAMPLE #3 - WITH CAPITAL IMPROVEMENTS

Same as Example #2, except that Adams made capital improvements of $30,000 using his own savings, by adding garages to each unit.   He then put these garages on his Depreciation Schedule, and he has taken $7,644 straight-line depreciation on them.

Does this change his tax liability?

RESULTS #3

Yes. These factors change the tax liability in the following ways.

DEPRECIATION

In previous Examples, he has taken $65,400 depreciation on the two units, and now he has taken $7,644 depreciation on the two garages, both straight-line, and his total is now $73,044.

BASIS

The basis in the property is the purchase price, plus any capital improvements, minus depreciation taken.   The basis is now $200,000 purchase price, plus $30,000 capital improvements, for a total of $230,000, minus $73,044 depreciation. His basis in the property is now $156,956.

CAPITAL GAINS

This is the difference between what the property sold for, and the basis. That number is now $400,000 minus $156,956. So, capital gains is now $243,044.

TAX LIABILITY

The portion of the $243,044 capital gains that is subject to depreciation recapture is now $73,044 and is still taxed at 25%, so this number is $18,261.

The remainder of the capital gains, $243,044 minus $73,044 depreciation, is $170,000, which you will notice is also the true difference between the Sale Price of $400,000 and what he paid for the property, $230,000 (200,000 purchase price plus 30,000 for two garages).

This $170,000 of true capital gains will be taxed at the capital gains rate of 20%. That number is $34,000.

The total tax liability is now $18,261 plus $34,000, which is $52,261.

EXAMPLE #4 - WITH PERSONAL PROPERTY

Same as Example #3, except that Adams decided two years ago to upgrade his units by removing all of the furniture and furnishings, and putting in all new furniture and furnishings, at a cost of $20,000 cash for both units combined. He had the opportunity to use accelerated depreciation to recover his investment quicker, so he chose the Double Declining Balance method and elected to take the Section 179 Bonus Depreciation the year he put the new assets in service, and he has claimed $15,200 in depreciation total in the two years.

How does this change his tax liability?

RESULTS #4

Adams has wandered into the tall weeds.

DEPRECIATION

He has previously taken $65,400 depreciation on the units, plus $7,644 depreciation on the garages, and now he has taken $15,200 depreciation on the furniture and furnishings. But this last item of depreciation is the problem.

The $65,400 and $7,644 are both straight-line depreciation and will be recaptured at the 25% rate that Adams must pay because of his marginal tax bracket of 39.6%.

But the $15,200 is not straight-line depreciation, it is accelerated depreciation, a method called Double Declining Balance, plus some Section 179 Bonus Depreciation.

The rule on accelerated depreciation is that the entire amount of depreciation taken, up to the total amount of the capital gains created by the transaction, must be recaptured at the ordinary income tax rate of the individual, in this case 39.6% for Adams.

This would result in a tax liability for Adams of $6,019 on the recapture of the $15,200 of accelerated depreciation that he took on the $20,000 of furniture and fixtures.

The rest of the factors you can compute for yourself using the same method we used in Example #3. Then check the Summary below to compare your numbers.

EXAMPLE #5 - WITH SECOND LIEN

Same as Example #4, except that Adams got a $30,000 home improvement loan to build the garages instead of using his own money. He put a second lien on the property, which was released when the loan was paid off at closing.

Does this change his tax liability?

RESULTS #5

No.

Since we are assuming a 20% capital gains tax rate and that number is constant for all of our Examples, the only other factors that affect the tax liability are:

* Purchase Price
* Capital Improvements
* Depreciation
* Basis (Purchase Price, plus Capital Improvements, minus Depreciation)
* Sales Price
* Amount of Capital Gains (Sales Price minus Basis)

It does not matter where he got the money to buy the property or where he got the money to make improvements to the property.

It does not matter how much of his proceeds are used to pay off loans.

And it does not matter what he does with the money that he takes away from the closing table.

SUMMARY

* Alan Adams bought a Duplex ten years ago for $200,000.
* He spent $50,000 on capital improvements (30,000 for the garages and 20,000 for the furniture and furnishings).

* He claimed $88,244 in depreciation.

* His Basis in the property is $161,756 (200,000 plus 50,000 minus 88,244).

* Bob Baker has offered him $400,000 for the Duplex.

* If he accepts, his Capital Gains will be $238,244 (400,000 Sale Price minus 161,756 depreciated basis).

* $15,200 of this will be Accelerated Depreciation Recapture, taxed at 39.6%, resulting in $6,019 tax.

* $73,044 of this will be regular depreciation recapture taxed at 25%, resulting in $18,261 tax.

* $150,000 will be regular capital gains (400,000 minus 250,000) and will be taxed at 20%, resulting in $30,000 tax.

* His total tax liability will be $54,280 ($6,019 plus $18,261 plus $30,000).

In the next chapter, Adams will figure out how to pay zero taxes.

Remember to register for free updates at:
www.S1031Exchange.com

You will also find expanded articles on all aspects of Section 1031 Like Kind Exchanges, and articles on related subjects like Leases, Contracts, and Real Estate Closings.

Chapter 3

SIMULTANEOUS EXCHANGE

SECTION 1031

Adams does not want to pay $54,280 in capital gains tax if he has another choice.

He has heard of the Section 1031 Like Kind Exchange, but he knows nothing about it, and mistakenly believes that "Exchange" means that he must trade his property with someone else who has property like his.

Proceeding on this mistaken assumption, he talks to Bob Baker, the Buyer, about making a trade, and learns that Baker also owns a warehouse with a fair market value of $400,000 which he would be willing to trade for the Duplex instead of paying cash for it.

Adams does not know if this property is "like" his, as in "Like Kind," and he also has other questions about the Exchange process. He realizes he needs to talk to someone called a Qualified Intermediary.

He has been told that having a Qualified Intermediary will provide him with a "safe harbor" with the IRS. He doesn't know what that is either, but he likes the sound of it.

SAFE HARBOR

The first time that you put together a deal that you know must later meet the approval of the IRS, you will feel like you're venturing out into shark-infested waters, in an untested craft, with no charts or maps, and no weather report.

It is not your imagination. That is exactly what you are doing.

But the IRS actually provides you with a "safe harbor" for the Section 1031 Like Kind Exchange transaction.

The requirements of Section 1031 are discussed in Treas. Reg. 1.1031(k)-1(g), which you can find in Appendix D, but which you don't need to read right now. Just understand that it establishes four situations under which the IRS will assume that you have met all of the requirements of Section 1031 in case they should look at your tax return, rather than asking you to prove everything.

The four situations are called "safe harbors."

One of the four is the use of a Qualified Intermediary.

QUALIFIED INTERMEDIARY

The Qualified Intermediary, which we will now refer to as QI, is often mistakenly described as the third party who takes title to the Exchangor's Relinquished Property from the Exchangor, then sells it, uses the proceeds to purchase the Replacement Property, and then deeds the Replacement Property to the Exchangor.

This is incorrect.

The QI never enters into the chain of title, and never becomes an agent for the Exchangor.

A QI is needed in the first place because the Exchangor can never have actual or "constructive" receipt of the funds from the sale of the Relinquished Property. "Constructive" receipt occurs when the Exchangor is able to control, direct, or exert influence over, the entity which actually receives his funds.

And although the most important business decision you will make is selecting your lawyer, the second most important, and critical, is your selection of a QI.

The QI is actually an independent entity which receives the Exchangor's funds from the sale of the Relinquished Property from the Title Company at closing, holds the funds, and then transfers them back to the Title Company to do the closing on the Exchangor's purchase of the Replacement Property. The Exchangor never receives or has control of the funds. The QI is paid by the Exchangor for this service. The cost is usually less than a thousand dollars.

Some taxpayers have suffered the consequences of just assuming that they can:

* sell the Relinquished Property,
* instruct the Title Company to hold their funds in the title company's escrow account instead of disbursing them,
* sign a contract to purchase the Replacement Property, and
* instruct the Title Company to use the escrowed funds to pay for the property at closing.

Why does this not work?

Because, under Section 1031, the taxpayer is not allowed to receive or have control over the net sales proceeds from the sale of the Relinquished Property.

In this case, the taxpayer obviously does have control over the proceeds because he is instructing the Title Company what to do with them. And the Title Company cannot refuse to give the funds to him if he asks.

You need a QI to handle the funds from the first sale.

But the QI will do more than that. It will also:

* Answer the Exchangor's questions about the Section 1031 Exchange process.

* Draft an "Exchange Agreement" between the Exchangor and the QI outlining exactly what will take place, and each party's rights and responsibilities.

* Review the sales contract concerning the Relinquished Property to make sure that the Exchangor's information is correct.

* Review the deed which originally put the Relinquished Property into the Exchangor's name to make sure that it is the same as the name on the sales contract, and that the property has been held for the required period of time.

* Provide the Exchangor with an Addendum to be added to the contract regarding the sale of the Relinquished Property, to be signed by the Buyer, acknowledging that the transaction is part of a 1031 Exchange and promising to cooperate, while being assured that there will be no additional cost or liability in doing so.

* Draft an "Assignment of Benefits" from the Exchangor to the QI of the Exchangor's contract to sell the Relinquished Property.

* Draft and send notices of the Assignment to all other parties to the contract, such as the real estate salesperson, the Title Company, and any financing entities.

* Open a bank account in the name of the Exchangor and with the Exchangor's social security number or federal tax identification number, usually a Qualified Escrow Account, but preferably a Qualified Trust Account. If the Exchangor will be providing more than the $250,000 amount that is the maximum insured by the FDIC, then multiple accounts will be opened.

* Review the Title Insurance Commitment to ensure that the information is correct.

* Review and approve the Title Company's proposed HUD-1 Settlement Statement.

* Review the proposed deed for the Relinquished Property for accuracy.

* Upon closing, receive the net sales proceeds from the Title Company and deposit them in the Exchangor's account or accounts.

* Provide a form on which the Exchangor will identify the potential Replacement Properties within 45 days after closing on the Relinquished Property, and verify that it is correct.

* When a contract is signed on one of the Replacement Properties, repeat all of the steps above.

* Monitor the 180-day time period for closing on the Replacement Property.

* When the closing is scheduled on the Replacement Property, transfer the Exchangor's funds to the Title Company to be used for purchasing the property.

* Provide the Exchangor an accounting of the entire transaction.

* Provide the Exchangor copies of all appropriate documents.

What the QI will not do is give you legal, financial, or tax advice, or negotiate on your behalf. They are not your agent, and they are not handling the deal for you. They are serving as an independent third party providing a professional service for your benefit.

Adams needs to find a QI who can do these things for him.

INTERVIEW

Adams realizes that the QI is now the most important person in his life, at least for the next six months.

When he begins his search for a QI, he knows that he will have to interview a number of them before he finds one that makes him feel comfortable, so he gets on the phone.

Adams: "Hello. I noticed from your website that you're a National Facilitator Organization member. What is that exactly?"

QI: "A NFO member is someone who specializes in handling Section 1031 Tax Free Exchanges."

Adams: "Tax free? Is that the same as a Like Kind Exchange?"

QI: "Same thing. That's what we call it."

Adams: "But it's not really tax free, is it, every time?"

QI: "If you don't pay taxes, it's tax free. It's one of the tax loopholes that turns ordinary investors into millionaires."

Adams: "Can you tell me how the process works?"

QI: "You can look on our website. We have an excellent explanation there."

Adams: "Yeah, I read that. It's a magazine article from 2001 written by a South Dakota attorney."

QI: "Not that much has changed. Look, you don't have to worry about any of this. Just turn it over to us."

Adams realizes he will not find a comfort zone with this one, so he calls the next QI on his list.

Adams: "Yeah, I'm planning on doing a 1031 Exchange, and I was wondering, can you tell me about your Certification, is that from the IRS?"

QI: "No."

Adams: "Is it from the federal government at all?"
QI: "No."
Adams: "State government?"
QI: "No."
Adams: "Is it a license of any kind, one you can lose?"
QI: "No."
Adams: "So, what is it?"
QI: "It's a Certificate."
Adams: "Issued by whom?"
QI: "The National Facilitators Organization."
Adams: "What did it cost?"
QI: "$299."
Adams: "I noticed that the name of your company has the word 'bank' in it. Are you a bank?"
QI: "No."

Adams figures that he will not find any comfort here either, so he goes on to the next QI on his list.

Adams: "I'm planning on doing a Section 1031 Exchange, selling my Duplex for $400,000 and I understand that I cannot receive or have any control over the funds, that they must be held by a Qualified Intermediary, and I wonder if you could tell me how that works?"
QI: "Well, the Title Company wires the funds to us and we hold them until you're ready to purchase your Replacement Property."
Adams: "How do you hold them?"
QI: "In the bank."
Adams: "In whose name?"
QI: "Ours."
Adams: "Does the bank know it's my money?"
QI: "That's not necessary."

Adams: "It sort of is. Is there any way the funds can be identified as mine?"

QI: "They are yours."

Adams: "I know that, and I hope that you know that, but they are in the bank in your name. What if something happens?"

QI: "Nothing will happen. We've been doing this a long time."

Adams: "Are you regulated or audited?"

QI: "That's not necessary."

Adams: "So if your secretary went to lunch and her purse was stolen and the account password was in her little notebook and someone stole the money, is there somebody who is going to replace my $400,000?"

QI: "We're bonded."

Adams: "Probably not for that. Anyway, let's say I'm ready to close, and the State puts a hold on your account because your bookkeeper has not been sending in the deductions from your employees' paychecks, and I miss my closing deadline and lose my tax-deferral."

QI: "That's not going to happen."

Adams: "Well, what if the local bank just didn't open up in the morning, how much of the $7 Million of other people's money in your account is insured by the FDIC?"

QI: "Would you like to talk to our attorney?"

Adams continues his search, and finds a QI that has offices in most major cities, managed by attorneys and accountants, who emphasize their professional status instead of a certificate they purchased, and who segregate the customer's account at the bank in the customer's own name and identification number in amounts covered by the FDIC guarantee.

EXCHANGE

Adams talks to his QI and learns that the "Exchange" in the title "Section 1031 Like Kind Exchange" does not mean exchange in the sense that he thought it did.

Instead of a "trade" or "swap" of a piece of property, it means more like taking one thing out and putting another thing in, such as "exchanging" one asset in an investment portfolio for another asset. The two pieces of property involved actually end up being owned by two other people who did not exchange anything with each other.

A better word for what actually happens would be "replacement." Adams is replacing one business asset or investment asset with another business asset or investment asset.

When trying to figure out the meaning of the tax laws, which we do constantly, we look at the Internal Revenue Code (IRC). Even though it is often unclear, and sometimes borders on gibberish, we have to use it because it is what the IRS uses. The best explanation of "exchange" that we have from the IRS is actually contained in another section of the Code that is referring to all of the exceptions contained in Section 1031.

Treasury Regulations Section 1.1002-1(c) concerning Sales and Exchanges says, "The underlying assumption... is that the new property is substantially a continuation of the old investment still unliquidated."

And this is the way that most real estate investors conduct their businesses. When they sell one investment that has gone up in value, of course they will use the money to get into another investment.

In the real world of day-to-day business, it is rare for two pieces of property to actually be traded for each other under Section

1031. Delayed Exchange Regulations were created in 1991, and provided all of the convenience and flexibility that are missing with a Simultaneous Exchange. Even Simultaneous Exchanges should probably be done as Delayed Exchanges because of the built-in flexibility. (Delayed Exchanges are discussed in the next chapter).

So, while Section 1031 does permit Adams to swap his $400,000 Duplex for Baker's $400,000 warehouse, this is not really what he wants to do. He wants to "exchange up" from his Duplex to a Fourplex, if he can find one, and he knows of about six of them that he might be able to buy, even if they are not on the market. However, the process might take some time.

His main concern at this point, though, is that he is not sure what kind of property he is permitted to choose as a Replacement Property once he has sold his Relinquished Property.

In other words, what does "like kind" really mean?

LIKE KIND

It is finally time to look at the actual language of the "INTERNAL REVENUE CODE SECTION 1031, EXCHANGE OF PROPERTY HELD FOR PRODUCTIVE USE OR INVESTMENT."

The first thing that we realize is that it is not really even called "Section 1031 Like Kind Exchange." But everyone, even the IRS, refers to it that way.

Section 1031(a)(1) reads as follows:

(a) Nonrecognition of Gain or Loss From Exchanges Solely in Kind.

(1) In General. - No gain or loss shall be recognized on the exchange of property held for productive use in a trade or business or for investment if such property is exchanged solely

for property of like kind which is to be held either for productive use in a trade or business or for investment.

Although it may not look like it, all of the information you need in order to understand the process is contained in that paragraph, and every word in it is important. Let's take it apart and look at it.

First, we need to determine what is meant by a "kind" of property and then which "kind" is "like" another "kind." Since we are primarily interested in real property, I can tell you up front that, for real estate investors, almost all real property can be like other real property for purposes of Section 1031, depending on your reason for owning it. But let's look at the code and regulations.

The IRS attempts an explanation in Treas. Reg. 1.1031(a) - 1(b) but it borders on being gibberish, and would not help us here, so we won't confuse things by looking at it. If you want to look at it, go to Appendix D.

Instead, let's break down Section 1031(a)(1) and find out what kind of property we are talking about. This is a slow and somewhat cumbersome explanation, but it is the best one available, and it will get us where we need to be.

Careful analysis will show that we are actually talking about only one "kind" of property, but there are two definitions of what "kind"(s) of property will go into that "category"/"kind."

Within the context of the paragraph, "kind" means

1. Property held for productive use in a trade or business and/or

2. Property held for investment.

So, we should not think about "kind" as in "What kind of property are you looking for, a house in a subdivision or a condo?"

Instead, we should think about "kind" as a category of property, as in "What kind of property are you investing in, rent houses or undeveloped land?" Think "category" instead of "kind."

"category" (of property)
1. held for productive use in a trade or business
    and/or
2. held for investment.

Therefore, any two properties are of a "like kind" if either is business property or investment property. It doesn't depend on what they look like or what purpose they serve, but depends on the reason you are owning them.

Look back at the explanation from Treas. Reg. 1.1002-1(c) above that says:

"The underlying assumption... is that the new property is substantially a continuation of the old investment still unliquidated."

Now, look back up above at the "held for" requirement in the Section 1031 text. This requirement refers to the Exchangor. It says "property held for productive use in a trade or business or held for investment." You can buy a house from someone, and for that person it doesn't meet either of these requirements because he is living in it. It is not "held for" business or "held for" investment. But after you buy it, you rent it out and collect income, and now it does meet the requirement of Section 1031(a)(1) because now it is "held for" "productive use in a trade or business" by you. It is the same property, but not the same in the hands of different owners because it is "held for" different purposes.

So, if you sell real property that you are holding for "productive use in a trade or business" or "for investment" and purchase property of equal or greater value using the net sales proceeds and intend to hold that property for "productive use in a trade or business" or "for investment," then you probably meet the requirements of Section 1031.

In fact, this whole area of tax law would probably all have been less confusing if the law had been called "Section 1031 Similar Category Replacement" instead of "Section 1031 Like Kind Exchange."

Adams is now getting excited about the prospect of being able to keep the $54,280 capital gains tax and reinvesting it, instead of sending it to the IRS, but realizes that he needs to go carefully, and now he is wondering how long he must hold property in order to meet the "held for" requirement in the law.

HELD FOR

Keep in mind that the Exchangor is the one who must qualify for tax deferral by complying with the terms of Section 1031. The other parties to the transaction, the Buyer of the Relinquished Property and the Seller of the Replacement Property, really don't have to do anything.

The Relinquished Property must be property that was "held for" business or investment by the Exchangor. This means that the Duplex which Adams owns and which he is planning to sell must be property which is being held by him for business or investment. Well, obviously it is, but then the question becomes "since when?"

In other words, how long must Adams have held the property as business or investment property in order for the property to qualify as Section 1031 property?

There is no answer. It is hard to believe, but there is no specified period set out in the Code or in the Treasury Regulations. And there are no U.S. Tax Court cases nor Federal District Court cases that supply the answer. This has been an ongoing question since Section 1031 first came into existence in the 1920's and the IRS has still not provided an answer.

All of the analysis that we can do leads to the conclusion that it is at least a year and a day, and a safe number is two years.

We know that the number is at least a year and a day because it must be at least a year and a day in order for the gain on the sale to be classified as long-term capital gains, which is what Section 1031 deals with. Section 1031 does not pertain to short-term capital gains, which would be taxed as ordinary income, because the IRS would never allow a taxpayer to defer taxes on ordinary income, even if it was reinvested. So, everyone agrees that the time period involved is at least a year and a day, in order to make it long-term capital gains.

There are some analysts who conclude that the time period is two years because there are some Tax Court case opinions regarding how long the Replacement Property must be held, and those opinions talk about "two tax years," meaning starting in one tax year and ending in another. But that analysis does not hold water because December 31 and January 1 could be in "two tax years" and yet only be one day apart.

I have read those opinions and I think it is possible the Court was talking about two complete 12-month "tax years," or tax reporting periods. In other words, the transaction takes place in one tax year and is reported on the tax return at the end of the year, and then is held for all or a portion of the next tax year, and the income is reported on the tax return at the end of that second tax year. That also bolsters the position that it must be at least a year and a day.

This does not mean that it must be rented for a year and a day in order to be investment property, but that it was available for rent during this period of time. So, if you buy a property and do some repairs before renting it, you should advertise it for rent immediately after you buy it, while you are doing the repairs, and sign a lease as soon as possible.

There are also some writers who have found court cases where an exchange was qualified by the Court even though the Exchangor had held the property for a few months. But that ruling pertained to those particular taxpayers with that particular set of facts, usually involving a hardship. The ruling did not say that everyone in the country can do the same thing. So, be very wary when you read about cases like this. Stick with at least a year and a day.

So, why doesn't the law contain a number that we can rely on? Well, instead of just picking a number, which the IRS and the Tax Court could easily do, they prefer to consider these matters in terms of the taxpayer's "intent" regarding the property, even though we all know that intent can never be determined with certainty at any point in time, and that it can change frequently. But that remains the IRS position on the question.

So, the holding period for the Relinquished Property should be at least a year and a day so that the disposition qualifies as long-term capital gains, and at least long enough after that so that the property appears on your tax return as being "held for productive use in a trade or business" if it is income property, and for a similar period if it is investment property.

The bottom line is that the holding period for the Replacement

Property should also be at least a year and a day, and long enough thereafter to convince the IRS that the intent when acquiring the property was that it was "to be held either for productive use in a trade or business or for investment."

So, in conclusion, one year and a day is a necessity, two years is a safe harbor, and anything in between is a personal decision.

RELATED PERSONS

One of the properties Adams is considering purchasing as a Replacement Property is owned by his parents. He knows that Section 1031 will not qualify transactions between "related persons" and he wonders if he can purchase a Replacement Property from his parents. The Buyer for his Duplex, Bob Baker, is actually his uncle, and the QI has already told him that this will not disqualify his transaction for Section 1031 treatment.

"Related Person" means your spouse, your brother, your sister, your parent, your grandparent, your child, and your grandchild.

It also includes a corporation or similar business entity in which you own more than 50% of the stock. This percentage includes your spouse's ownership. It also includes a Partnership and a Limited Liability Company in which you and your spouse own an interest of more than 50%. It also includes trusts and estates, with complex rules.

"Related Person" does not include an in-law, an aunt, an uncle, a cousin, a nephew, a niece, and an ex-spouse.

So, Adams can sell his Relinquished Property to Bob Baker, his uncle, because an uncle is not a Related Person.

But the answer to the question of whether two Related Persons can enter into a 1031 Exchange with each other is "yes" and "no."

Related Persons can do a direct swap of properties, and that transaction will qualify as a Section 1031 Exchange for one or both of them, but each of them must then hold onto their acquired property for a period that is more than two years after the date of the last transfer which was part of the Exchange. If either person violates this requirement, the 1031 Exchange is invalidated, with taxes and interest and penalties assessed, for both of them. Each person who qualified the transaction as a 1031 Exchange must continue to file Form 8824 for two years following the year of the Exchange. (Form 8824 is the IRS Form that the Exchangor must file to report the Section 1031 Like Kind Exchange. It is covered in Chapter 7).

And also, in addition to the direct swap, the Exchangor can sell the Relinquished Property to a Related Person. But the Related Person is required to hold the property for the two-year period described above, and failing to do so will invalidate the Section 1031 Exchange for the Exchangor. And the Exchangor is held to the same filing requirements of Form 8824 described above, except that it might turn into three years because the period will start to run from the date he acquires the Replacement Property, which could be as long as 180 days after the first transaction.

The exception to the two-year holding requirement is in the event of death or other involuntary conversion.

So, two Related Persons can swap properties. And Adams can sell his Relinquished Property to a Related Person.

The real danger here is in buying the Replacement Property from a Related Person. It is not absolutely prohibited, but it guarantees that the IRS will look closely at the transaction. For that reason, you absolutely should not do it.

There is no single "rule" that we can look at to see the IRS position on this. There are a series of court decisions that make up the position of the IRS.

But if there was a rule, it would say that the IRS just doesn't like it when one Related Person ends up with the property and the other Related Person ends up with the cash.

Apparently, the IRS is very conscious of property being shifted from a high-tax taxpayer to a low-tax taxpayer, and the IRS believes that it is more likely that family members will collude with each other to circumvent the rules, more than people who are not related. I have not found that to be the case.

Now, despite their attitude, the IRS has actually permitted an Exchangor acquiring the Replacement Property from a Related Person, when the Related Person is also doing a 1031 Exchange, and does not keep the cash received from the Exchangor, but uses it to acquire a Replacement Property.

What you must remember is that the IRS is fighting a battle here against taxpayers who are trying to "game" the system, and you probably do not want to put yourself in with that group, and have your tax return pulled and examined every year.

TIME LINE #1: 45 DAYS

So, where are we?

Adams has
* found a buyer for his Duplex for $400,000,
* estimated his capital gains tax to be $54,280,
* verified that his transaction will qualify for a 1031 Exchange,
* made sure that he is entering into a "safe harbor" transaction,
* found a QI to guide him through the process,
* learned what "exchange" really means,
* learned what "kind" means,
* learned what "like kind" means,

* learned who he can sell to, and from whom he can buy, and
* learned the periods for which each property must be held.

As we discussed, in the modern business world today, no one tries to do a Simultaneous Exchange, and for two reasons:
* it is almost impossible to make two things happen simultaneously, and
* it is not necessary to even try, because the rules for a Delayed Exchange are very clear, easy to follow, and provide almost total flexibility.

So, since Adams will be doing a Delayed Like Kind Exchange, he is ready to lay out his time line for the entire transaction.

The first time period involved in a Section 1031 Exchange is the 45-day time period.

The time starts to run on the Exchange Date. This is the date on which the Exchangor transfers the Relinquished Property to the Buyer. If the 1031 Exchange involves two pieces of Relinquished Property, the time starts to run on the first Exchange Date.

A "transfer" occurs on the earlier of the date the Exchangor signs the document evidencing the transfer (usually a deed), or the date the document is filed in the public records. The date that is normally used is the date on the Title Company's HUD-1 Settlement Statement, which will usually be the day the transaction closed.

During the 45-day period, the Exchangor must identify the possible properties that he will acquire as Replacement Property. He identifies them to his QI, who documents the action for IRS purposes.

He can identify 3 possible properties without regard to the fair market value of each one, or the total fair market value of all three. Remember, what he buys must be of a value equal to, or greater than, the sales price of what he is selling. In other words, the Purchase Price of the Replacement Property must be at least equal to the Sales Price of the Relinquished Property.

Or, he can identify more than 3 possible properties, and state the fair market value of each one, provided their combined fair market value is not more than 200% of the fair market value of the Relinquished Property. In other words, he could sell an apartment building for $1,000,000 and identify 40 rent houses with an average fair market value of $50,000 each, totaling $2,000,000. Not that he would, but that is how this second option works.

There is a third option which no one ever uses, because it makes no sense, so I won't go into it.

The Replacement Property should be identified with sufficient detail to distinguish it from any other piece of property. Adams can use the street address, or the lot and block, or the surveyor's legal description, or even the unique number assigned to the parcel by the property-taxing authority. The legal description is the best choice, the lot and block is second-best, and the street address is least-best. Another choice, the number assigned to the property by the local taxing authority, should not be used because it is unreliable and often incorrect.

In addition to identifying the real property, Adams is also probably required to identify the personal property that will complete the exchange, but this can be more general, since file cabinets or refrigerators or dairy cows are really "fungibles," the items are interchangeable with another of the same description.

After the Exchangor creates his list and provides it to his QI, he can make changes to it during the 45-day period, but it is set on the last day, and cannot be changed after that. We should note that the Replacement Property can actually be more than one piece of property, as can the Relinquished Property, and can be mixed, investment and business properties. We will discuss this more at the appropriate time.

As I said, the identification is made by the Exchangor to the QI, who will document it in writing with the appropriate signatures.

The Exchange Date that we are using in our Examples is January 1, 2017. That means that Day 1 is January 2, and Day 30 is January 31, and Day 45 is February 15. So the Exchangor must present the list to the QI on or before February 15.

Anyone who waits until the last day is asking for trouble. Allow yourself 30 days to identify these possible properties, and then you have another 15 days to deal with any unforeseen problems that might arise, and make changes.

Of course, if you acquire your Replacement Property within the 45-day period, the Exchange is complete and there is no need to identify the property to the QI.

TIME LINE #2: 180 DAYS

The second time period involved in a Section 1031 Exchange is the 180-day time period.

The time starts to run on the Exchange Date, just like the 45-day time period.

The 180-day time period is the time period in which the Exchangor must acquire the Replacement Property.

If the Exchange Date is in one tax year, say on December 21, and the 180-day period extends into the following year, which it would, beyond the day that the entity's tax return is due, say April 15 if it is an individual, then the period terminates on the due date of the tax return, which would be 115 days after December 21, instead of 180, unless the due date of the tax return is extended. So, the rule is either 180 days, or the due date, including extensions, of the tax return covering the period in which any part of the transaction occurred, whichever comes first.

Our Exchange Date is January 1, 2017 and the 180-day period expires in June 30, 2017. It is not necessary for us to get an extension for the tax return due in March or April of 2017 because it is not the tax return on which this transaction will be reported.

CONCLUSION

Adams now has all of the information he needs to select his Replacement Property.

He is ready to start his Section 1031 Like Kind Exchange.

* Alan Adams bought a Duplex ten years ago for $200,000.

* He has taken $65,400 straight-line depreciation on the units.

* He spent $30,000 capital improvements on two garages.

* He has taken $7,644 straight-line depreciation on the garages.

* He spent $20,000 on new furniture and furnishings.

* He has taken $15,200 accelerated depreciation on them.

* His total amount of capital improvements is $50,000 ($30,000 + $20,000)

* His total depreciation is $88,244 ($65,400 + $7,644 + $15,200).

* His basis in the property is $161,756 ($200,000 + $50,000 - $88,244).

* Bob Baker has offered him $400,000 cash for the Duplex.

* $161,756 of this will represent his depreciated basis in the property.

* His capital gains will be $238,244 ($400,000 - $161,756).

* His tax liability on the $238,244 will be $54,280.

* $15,200 accelerated depreciation recapture will be taxed at 39.6%. ($6,019).

* $73,044 regular depreciation recapture will be taxed at 25%. ($18,261).

* $150,000 regular capital gains will be taxed at 20%. ($30,000).

In Chapter 4 we will cover the most common type of Section 1031 Exchange, the Delayed Like Kind Exchange, and look at eight possible transactions that Adams can enter into in order to defer payment of the capital gains tax of $54,280 and how the numbers will lay out for him in each one.

Author's Note:

The following Chapter 4 is the most important one in the book. When you understand this, everything else will fall into place.

Chapter 4

DELAYED EXCHANGE

EXAMPLE #1 - NET SALES PROCEEDS

Adams wants to "exchange up" from his $400,000 Duplex, and he is now looking for a Fourplex to buy as his Replacement Property. He found seven different Fourplexes in his area that were not listed for sale, and talked to the owners. Three of the owners were interested enough to show him the properties and invite him to make an offer.

He has not identified the three properties to his QI as part of his obligation to do so within the 45-day rule because he has not closed on selling his Relinquished Property, and the 45 days have not started to run. His Buyer for the Relinquished Property, Bob Baker, has presented him with a signed sales contract with an Earnest Money check attached, and Adams has three weeks to sign the contract and accept, and then the contract provides for a closing date within thirty days, but with conditions to delay it by either party. So Adams has built in plenty of flexibility for himself in finding his Replacement Property.

All three of the properties he is considering are appraised on the property tax rolls at about $700,000 and Adams has talked to his loan officer and the bank is willing to loan up to $560,000 on the one he decides to buy. Adams has a good loan history and payment history with the bank.

Adams is very excited. He knows that the price of the Replacement Property must be equal to or greater than the Selling Price of the Relinquished Property, and all of these properties meet that qualification.

He is still learning how the process works, with the help of his QI, and thinks he only needs to reinvest his $238,244 capital gains, using that as a Down Payment if he takes out the loan, since the other $161,756 of the net sales proceeds represents the return to him of what is left of his original purchase price for the Relinquished Property, and that he will get it back. He is thinking about buying a boat with that $161,756. A really nice boat.

He contacts his QI to discuss his plans, and finds out that this is not going to happen the way he thought.

REPLACEMENT PROPERTY

To be completely tax deferred, all of the net sales proceeds that the Exchangor is entitled to receive from the sale of the Relinquished Property at closing must be used to purchase the Replacement Property. The Exchangor cannot receive any of the money. The Section 1031 Exchange process will, in effect, convert the equity in the current investment into cash, and put all of the cash inside the next investment.

Adams thought he only had to reinvest his $238,244 in capital gains, but he learns that he must also reinvest the rest of it, the $161,756 that represents his basis in the Relinquished Property. In other words, the entire $400,000 of net sales proceeds from the sale of the property must be put into the Replacement Property.

That means that he will have a $400,000 down payment, and that he will be getting a bank loan for $300,000.

And that brings up another subject that should be discussed.

In addition to the requirement that the Replacement Property must be of equal or greater value than the Relinquished Property, and the requirement that all cash received from the sale of the Relinquished Property ("net sales proceeds") must be put into the Replacement Property, there is a third requirement that everyone talks about that is not really a requirement at all, and you should not be sidetracked by it if you see it mentioned somewhere.

The confusion comes from an incorrect reading of Treas. Reg. 1.1031(d) - 2 which talks about "Treatment of Assumption of Liabilities."

Some people mistakenly believe that this section requires that the debt placed on the Replacement Property (the money you borrow to purchase it) must be at least equal to the debt paid off on the Relinquished Property, or the difference must be made up by adding cash.

Now, let's look at this a little closer and see if it makes sense.

Assume a situation where someone sold a rent house for $100,000 and paid off a loan of $99,000. They received $1,000 cash and this must be reinvested. But they must purchase a replacement property for at least $100,000 to qualify for a Section 1031 Exchange, so they must either:

* get a new loan for $99,000 to go with their net sales proceeds of $1,000 or
* use $99,000 of their own money or
* some combination of new loan and new cash.

So, the very dynamics of the deal will require that they either get new financing equal to the debt that was paid off, or add their own money. There's no other way it will work. So, it is not really a "requirement" of Section 1031, it is going to have to happen anyway.

I hope that is not confusing. But it comes up all of the time, and is usually explained incorrectly. I just didn't want you to get hung up in this.

As I've said before, in computing your capital gains, the IRS does not care where you get the money you bring to the table, and it doesn't care what debts are paid off from your sales proceeds. As long as you use all of your net sales proceeds, and buy a property of equal or greater value, you will have to get a new loan at least equal to the other, or use your own cash. So, it is not a requirement, it is just a necessity. You don't even have to get a new loan, you can use your own cash. The IRS is not in the business of forcing you to get a bank loan.

Now, let's see what Adams's transaction looks like in real numbers.

RESULTS #1

Adams buys the Fourplex for $700,000.

His QI wires the $400,000 that he is holding from the sale of the Relinquished Property to the Title Company.

At closing, Adams signs the bank's loan documents for $300,000 and the bank wires those funds to the Title Company.

The Title Company gives the $700,000 to the Seller of the Fourplex.

Adams now owns the Replacement Property.

At this point we need to discuss briefly what the IRS calls "Elections."

In some situations you are given the choice of doing things one way or doing them another way. The IRS doesn't care, they just want you to commit to whatever you are doing so that you can be held to it.

Concerning the Replacement Property, Adams has the choice of continuing to depreciate his basis of $161,756 in the Relinquished Property, even though he no longer owns it, because the basis has now been transferred into the Replacement Property, and he will refer to it on his Depreciation Schedule as "Old Basis," and then, he can begin depreciating his basis in the Replacement Property of $300,000 representing his bank loan, and refer to it on his Depreciation Schedule as "New Basis."

In fact, the Income Tax Regulations assume that Adams will continue to handle his depreciation in this manner unless he makes an "Election" to roll the basis in the Relinquished Property into the Replacement Property along with his newly-created basis there, and start a new Depreciation Schedule for the Replacement Property for the entire $461,756 less $40,000 which he will allocate to the land.

On Form 4562, filed with his Form 1040 for the first tax year in which he owns the Replacement Property, Adams will make the election by checking the box that says "Election Made Under Section 1.168(i)-6T(i)."

Then his $161,756 basis in the Relinquished Property is transferred as basis to the Replacement Property. But it is increased by the amount of new money he put into the property, the $300,000, to make his total basis now $461,756 in the

Replacement Property. Another way to compute his basis in the Replacement Property, and arrive at the same number, is to take the price he paid, and subtract the amount of capital gains that was deferred, $700,000 minus $238,244. It is still $461,756. He will assign a $40,000 value to the land, and begin depreciating the remaining $421,756 immediately for the 27.5 year period, and his depreciation allowance will be $1,278 per month, or $15,337 per year.

The $238,244 capital gains, which he did not pay taxes on, also transfers to the new property simply as tax-deferred capital gains, and the number will reside there inside the Replacement Property until he does another Section 1031 Exchange and it is increased by the deferred amount involved in the new transaction, or he makes it go away, which I will explain to you later.

All of these numbers are in simplified form. I am aware that they do not reflect a "real world" transaction. I have used them for the purpose of explaining the concept of the transactions in the simplest way possible.

Now that you understand the concepts, we will start using the more realistic numbers and situations that you are likely to encounter in your own transaction.

EXAMPLE #2 - PARTIALLY TAX DEFERRED

We have been talking about everything that Adams must do to qualify for a Section 1031 Exchange, and the Exchange we have been talking about, of course, is an Exchange that is completely tax deferred.

But Adams might want to consider an exchange in which part of the Exchange is tax deferred, and part of the Exchange is taxable.

This is permitted under Section 1031, it is simple enough to do, and it will not endanger the entire Exchange.

Suppose that Adams will be involved in a different transaction during the same tax year in which he is selling a capital asset at a loss. If that loss is a long-term capital loss, and he has no other long-term capital gains to subtract it from, he will not be allowed to subtract that loss from the rest of his ordinary income, he will only be permitted to deduct $3,000 of the long-term capital loss on his tax return this year, and each succeeding year. The reason for this is that he would be deducting a capital loss which, if it were a capital gain, would be taxed at 20%, from ordinary income. The IRS does not like for taxpayers to deduct capital losses from ordinary income because they involve two different tax brackets, and amounts of cash. Capital gains income is taxed at a maximum of 20% and ordinary income is taxed at a maximum of 39.6%.

So, let's assume that Adams has an asset that has gone down $100,000 in value that he would like to sell if he can get some benefit from doing so.

He can take $100,000 cash at closing on the sale of the Relinquished Property and have the other $300,000 of his net sales proceeds sent by the Title Company to the QI, and increase his bank loan to $400,000.

How will this change the transaction?

RESULTS #2

Since the contract to sell the Replacement Property has been assigned to the QI, it is the QI who will deal with the Title Company, and instruct them to disburse $100,000 of the net sales proceeds to Adams, and instruct them to wire the remaining funds to the QI.

At the closing, Adams will receive a Cashiers Check for $100,000 and this portion of his net sales proceeds will be subject to long-term capital gains tax, and he can still qualify the other $138,244 of his capital gains for tax deferral treatment.

He has already met the first qualification of Section 1031 by not touching the other $300,000.

And he plans to purchase a Replacement Property for $700,000, which is equal to or greater than the $400,000 net sales proceed from the Relinquished Property.

By the way, the "net sales proceeds" is not capital gains plus transferred basis in the property. If some of what he is entitled to get is used to pay off a mortgage, that amount is deducted to determine the net sales proceeds.

His next qualification for complete tax deferral is that he must put all of the net sales proceeds of $400,000 into the Replacement Property. But he cannot do this, because the QI is only holding $300,000 of the $400,000 net sales proceeds.

Therefore the Section 1031 Exchange will only defer taxes on the $138,244 of the capital gains that is part of the $300,000 that he does reinvest in the Replacement Property. The other $100,000 that Adams received at closing will be taxable to Adams.

So we now need to determine how that $100,000 will be taxed.

If Adams has another transaction in which he incurs a $100,000 long-term capital loss, this loss will offset the gain when both are reported on his Schedule D, and the $100,000 will not be taxed at all.

Another possibility is that Adams has been operating the Duplex at a loss but he is a high-income individual, which he is, and has not been permitted to deduct the losses and has "Suspended Passive Activity Losses" that he can deduct from the $100,000. If you are in this situation you must have your tax professional walk you through the steps.

But if Adams does not have a $100,000 capital loss to use to offset the taxes, and he just wanted the money to buy a boat and is willing to pay taxes on the money, how will the $100,000 be taxed? At the 20% capital gains rate?

Well, the $400,000 that he received from the sale represented his $161,756 basis left in the property, that is transferring to the Replacement Property, plus his $238,244 capital gains on the deal. So, which one of those does his $100,000 belong in?

It is the position of the IRS that when you receive money from the sale of a capital asset, the first dollar you get represents your profit, and continues until all of the profit is accounted for, and then the next dollar you receive represents the return of your investment. So the $100,000 will not be deducted from his basis. It will be considered part of his capital gains of $238,244 and he will have to report it as a capital gain.

Then we have the question of what does the $100,000 represent in terms of income; that is, which income tax bracket this $100,000 is in.

We know that the $100,000 he received is part of his $238,244 capital gains, which was actually broken down as $150,000 true capital gains, $73,044 straight-line depreciation recapture, and $15,200 accelerated depreciation recapture.

And remember that true capital gains is taxed at 20%, Section 1250 Depreciation Recapture (straight-line) is taxed at 25%, and accelerated depreciation recapture is taxed at the taxpayer's ordinary income tax rate, which is 39.6% for Adams.

Now, here is a rule that you need to always remember. It is the position of the IRS that when taxes are assessed on a "bundle" of income, like deferred capital gains in this instance, they start with collecting the highest tax first.

So, $15,200 accelerated depreciation will be taxed at 39.6%, which is $6,019.

The $73,044 of straight-line depreciation will be taxed at 25%, which is $18,261.

And the remaining $11,756 of the $100,000 that he received will be considered pure capital gains, and taxed at 20%, which is $2,351.

His total tax on the $100,000 is $26,631, which turns out to be an effective tax rate of 26.6%. He would only end up with $73,369 of the $100,000 in his pocket.

Now, back to the other numbers.

His basis in the Replacement Property will be $561,756 which will be the $161,756 carried over from the Relinquished Property plus the new $400,000 borrowed from the bank and used in the purchase. His loan went up from $300,000 to $400,000 because he took out the $100,000 at closing.

He must now assign $40,000 to the value of the land, leaving $521,756 depreciable basis in the new property.

His depreciation allowance will be $1,581 per month, or $18,973 per year.

His yearly depreciation allowance actually went up by $3,636 because he took out the $100,000 of profit and borrowed that much more.

(Notice that $3,636 multiplied by 27.5 years equals $100,000.)

EXAMPLE #3 - A TYPICAL TRANSACTION

We are now at the point where we understand the Section 1031 Exchange process well enough to start using real numbers and real situations, those that are likely to occur in your own transaction.

The Examples will gradually become more complex, but because you understand the basic concepts, they will not become more complicated for you.

RELINQUISHED PROPERTY

* Adams bought a Duplex ten years ago for $200,000.

* The price was allocated $20,000 land and $180,000 building.

* The furniture and furnishings were of negligible value, none assigned.

* He put the building on his Depreciation Schedule at $180,000 for 27.5 years.

* He has taken $65,400 straight-line depreciation on the building.

* He spent $30,000 capital improvements on two garages.

* He borrowed the $30,000 from the bank and put a lien on the property.

* The balance of the note is now $18,000.

* He has taken $7,644 straight-line depreciation on the garages.

* He spent $20,000 cash on new furniture and furnishings.

* He has taken $15,200 accelerated depreciation on them.

* His capital improvements total is $50,000 ($30,000 + $20,000).

* His total depreciation is $88,244 ($65,400 + $7,644 + $15,200).

* His basis in the property is $161,756 ($200,000 + $50,000 - $88,244).

* Bob Baker, the Buyer, has offered $400,000 cash for the Duplex.

* His total costs of the sale will be $10,000 closing costs.

REPLACEMENT PROPERTY

* Adams has found a Fourplex to purchase from Carl Carter for $700,000 cash.

* The value of the land is $40,000.

* The value of the furniture and furnishings is $20,000.

* His total other costs of acquisition will be $5,000 closing costs.

RESULTS #3

There are a number of questions to be answered with this transaction.

1.) IS THIS PROPERTY "LIKE KIND" PROPERTY?

The first question to answer in any Section 1031 Exchange is whether the Replacement Property is "like kind."

We are tempted to say that it is, because it is just a bigger building of the same type, and because the current owner is holding it "for productive use in a trade or business."

But this is not the correct analysis.

The language of Section 1031 says that for the Exchangor, the Replacement Property must be "property of a kind which is to be held either for productive use in a trade or business or for investment."

In other words, it does not matter at all what the Seller is doing with the property. Since the Seller is not a Related Person, he has nothing to do with whether or not the Exchangor can qualify this property for a Section 1031 Exchange.

In this Example, Adams intends to continue with the rental activities when he becomes the owner of the Fourplex, and that is all he must do in order to qualify the Replacement Property as "like kind." That shows his "intent." Of course, he must continue that for at least a year, and preferably two.

So, yes, the property is "like kind" property.

2.) IS THE REPLACEMENT PROPERTY PRICED HIGH ENOUGH?

The next question is whether the Replacement Property Price is equal to, or greater than, the sales price from the Relinquished Property.

We know by looking at the numbers that it is, but we always do the math.

The sales price will be the Gross Sales Price of $400,000 minus the cost of the transaction, which is the $10,000 closing costs. So Adams will net $390,000.

The Replacement Property Price will be the Gross Purchase Price plus any other costs of acquisition, which will be the $5,000 closing costs. So the Replacement Property Price is $705,000.

The Replacement Property Price is greater than the net sales price of the Relinquished Property.

3.) HOW MUCH CASH MUST ADAMS PUT INTO THE DEAL?

This is not the question of how much the net sales price will be.

This is a question of how much money Adams will be entitled to receive at the end of closing, which will be wired to his QI, and become the amount that the QI wires back to the Title Company to be used in the purchase of the Replacement Property when that transaction takes place. Remember, the Exchangor, Adams, cannot receive or have constructive receipt of any of the money if he wants the entire transaction to be tax deferred. So, the quick answer to how much cash (from the sale) Adams must put into the deal is "all of it."

But we still need to arrive at the number. To compute this number, take the $400,000 and subtract the $10,000 closing costs, like we just did, and get $390,000. But this is not the answer.

Adams would not be getting this amount if this were a regular sale without an exchange, because he must pay off a debt on the property, which was originally $30,000, used to build the garages, and which he has paid down to $18,000.

So the amount of cash that Adams would be entitled to receive at closing is $400,000 minus $10,000 minus $18,000, or $372,000. This is the "net sales proceeds" and this is the amount that he must put into the Replacement Property.

That also means that his new loan amount will probably be $333,000.

4.) WHAT IS THE CAPITAL GAINS?

We know that Adams' basis in the property is what he paid for it, plus his capital improvements, minus his depreciation taken. This number is $161,756 ($200,000 + $50,000 - $88,244). So his capital gains would be the net sales proceeds of $390,000 ($400,000 sales price - $10,000 closing cost) minus his basis of $161,756, or $228,244.

When this total capital gains number of $228,244 is carried over into the Replacement Property, it will retain the individual breakdown identifications of:

  * $140,000 actual capital gains ($390,000 net proceeds - $250,000 cost plus improvements),
  * $73,044 straight-line depreciation recapture, and
  * $15,200 accelerated depreciation recapture.

5.) WHAT IS THE CARRYOVER BASIS, AND THE NEW BASIS?

The basis in the Relinquished Property is $161,756 so this will be carried over into the Replacement Property.

The capital gains is $228,244 and this will be carried over into the new property.

The rest of the $705,000 will be made up of newly created basis, or $315,000, which is the difference between the $705,000 purchase price of the Replacement Property and the $390,000 net sale proceeds on the sale of the Relinquished Property. Another way to look at it is the new loan of $333,000 less the $18,000 of debt paid off.

The way I like to compute it is to take the $705,000 paid for the Replacement Property and take out the $161,756 that represents the transferred basis from the Relinquished Property, and then take out the $228,244 that represents the amount of the capital gains on the sale of the Relinquished Property that was deferred by transferring it into the Replacement Property, and you have $315,000 left. This is the amount of basis created in the Replacement Property.

Add this newly-created basis of $315,000 to the transferred basis of $161,756 and you have a new basis of $476,756, including land and building.

EXCEPT THAT IT IS EVEN MORE COMPLICATED THAN THIS!

Now, stay with me on 6.), we can work through it.

This will give you an understanding of the role that personal property plays in the Section 1031 Exchange. And understanding the role that personal property plays in the overall transaction can save you more money than all of your other wheeling and dealing. It's knowledge you'll use daily for the rest of your life.

6.) WHAT ABOUT THE PERSONAL PROPERTY?

Almost every transaction is made up of both real property and personal property. "Personal property" as used here doesn't mean your fishing equipment or your hair dryer, not that kind of "personal." The IRS divides assets into "real property" and "depreciable tangible personal property" (and others, but we will focus on these two). The "personal property" that we are dealing with is the furniture and furnishings in the two properties, both the Relinquished Property and the Replacement Property. It is actually business property in our minds because it is being used in a business to create income, but the IRS calls it personal property, so we have to do the same. It is property on which you claimed a depreciation deduction from income. Simply put, if it is part of the investment property, and it isn't real property, the IRS calls it personal property.

If your Section 1031 Exchange involves personal property, it must be "like kind" just like the real property does. But, while almost all real property can be "like" other real property, personal property is never "like" other personal property. See Chapter 10 for more information on personal property.

Also, you must acquire new personal property that is not only "like" the personal property that you sold, but also of a value equal to, or greater than, the personal property that you sold.

And it must be accounted for separately.

If you don't document the transaction in this manner, and the IRS later audits this transaction, they can attach any numbers they want to the personal property for valuation and you will have to accept them. And don't expect their numbers to be reasonable, or even make sense, because they never do.

On the other hand, this is an excellent opportunity for you to avoid a higher tax liability in favor of a lower tax liability.

Here's how that would be done.

For the first transaction involving the Relinquished Property, Adams would do a Deed to Baker, without a price recited, but would represent $395,200, for the building and the land, i.e, the real property. And then he would do a Bill of Sale to Baker for the furniture and furnishings with a recited price of $4,800 which is Adams's basis remaining in the furniture and furnishings. This way Adams will not have a capital gains on the personal property to report separately from the rest of the assets for recapture purposes, and can report them all together.

The advantage will come for Adams when he purchases the Replacement Property from Carter.

He will have Carter do a Deed to him, without a stated price, but which represents $680,000, for the building and land, the real property. And then he will have Carter sign a Bill of Sale to him for the furniture and furnishings for a price of $20,000.

This means that he will be able to depreciate this $20,000 of his investment over five years as "residential rental furnishings," instead of 27.5 years, like the building, and thereby generate more depreciation to shield more of his ordinary income from taxes much sooner.

Since he is purchasing like kind personal property of equal or greater value than the personal property he sold, he has not jeopardized his Section 1031 Exchange.

Another part of the Internal Revenue Code, Section 1060, permits the parties involved to assign these values in transactions involving both real and personal property.

7.) WHAT DOES THE NEW DEPRECIATION SCHEDULE LOOK LIKE?

One of the major considerations in any investment decision, including this one, is how much depreciation will be available to shield your ordinary income, including the rental income, from taxes. Since depreciation is not an out-of-pocket expense, it really just represents how much of the rent money you can put in your pocket without paying taxes.

For example, if your rental property shows income of $5,000 after deducting all out-of-pocket expenses but before you deduct depreciation, you would be sending almost $2,000 of that in taxes to the IRS, leaving $3,000 for you. But if your depreciation allowance is $5,000 for that property for that year, then you deduct that depreciation and pocket $5,000 instead of $3,000. That's 67% more.

For the Replacement Property, we start with the price of $705,000.

We have allocated $40,000 of this to land value, which is not depreciated, and that leaves $665,000.

Then we separate out the $20,000 that we have identified as the purchase price of the furniture and furnishings. It is not a new asset, so it will not qualify for Section 179 Bonus Depreciation, but Adams can depreciate this over a five-year period using the Double Declining Balance method and the MQ1 convention, and claim $7,000 the first year and $5,200 the second year.

The basis in the new building that we computed above was $476,756 but we have decided to sell the furniture and furnishings for $4,800 with a Bill of sale, and that leaves us a basis of $471,956.

But we have now decided to use $20,000 of the net sales proceeds to purchase the furniture and furnishings of the new Fourplex, so we must subtract that from the new computed basis, and we have $451,956. After assigning a $40,000 value to the land, we have a depreciable basis of $411,956.

This is the amount that Adams will be depreciating over the 27.5 year period. He will be able to claim $14,980.22 per year.

Adams will be able to deduct $1,248.35 per month in depreciation on the building and $583.33 per month on the furnishings ($433.33 the second year). In other words, that much of his monthly income will be tax free.

EXAMPLE #4 - ASSUMPTION OF DEBT

The lending rules that commercial banks and some other lenders must follow are very different from what they were a few years ago.

As a result, it is rare to have a transaction in which an existing mortgage, or any debt financing, is assumed by the purchaser, and also rare to have a bank agree to finance a purchase where the seller has taken back a note.

But there are still some rare situations where it might occur, so we will cover an example here and look at the Section 1031 rules that are in play.

Assume the same scenario as in the prior Example #3, except that:

* instead of Adams paying off the $18,000 balance due on his bank loan at closing, that mortgage was assumed by Baker, and

* when Adams purchased his Replacement Property, the Seller, Carl Carter, had a mortgage on the property with a balance of $100,000 and Adams agreed to assume that note and pay $600,000 cash.

Remember, this is highly unlikely, but the IRS uses examples like this often, so this will help you understand those examples.

RESULTS #4

The first item to look at here is the question of to whom Adams owes the note with a balance of $18,000 that Baker will assume. In other words, who is the Payee in the Note? And since the note will certainly have a "due on sale" clause, will the Payee agree to allow the new owner to assume the note?

The Note was originally in the amount of $30,000 and the lender was a bank, so the bank was the Payee. This could be a problem. That bank obviously qualified Adams as the borrower of the $30,000 at the time the loan was made, and Adams has been making payments for ten years.

But what about Baker? The bank doesn't know whether or not he is a responsible or credit-worthy person, and if they plan to go through the process of qualifying him as a borrower so that he can assume the note, they will probably just insist that he get a new loan. The process is almost the same. But this could delay the transaction, and if he does not qualify, it could jeopardize the deal.

But more importantly, if Baker also plans to get a loan for all or most of the remaining $382,000 of the purchase price, the new lender will want a first lien on the property. That means that the bank holding the original $30,000 note with a balance owed of $18,000 will not only have to agree to let Baker assume the note, but will also have to agree to "subordinate" the first lien status of the note to second lien status, that is, put it behind the new note for collection purposes because the new note will be a first lien note.

This would mean that if Baker defaulted on the new first lien note of $382,000 and the property is foreclosed on, the proceeds of the foreclosure sale will first go to the holder of the new first lien note. If there are any funds left over, they will go to the holder of the second lien note, the original $30,000 note with a balance owed of $18,000. There are never any funds left over. If the property is worth more than $400,000 the owner would sell it and pay off the notes instead of letting it be foreclosed on.

As you can see, there is about zero chance of the original lender agreeing to reduce his first lien to a second lien.

You can make the same analysis regarding Adams assuming the $100,000 note of Carter's on the Replacement Property, and come to the same conclusion.

But, what if, by some miracle, the two assumptions did occur?

How do these two assumptions affect the Section 1031 Exchange numbers?

In practical terms, Baker's assumption of Adams's note is the same as Baker giving $18,000 to Adams, and Adams paying off the note. Adams no longer has the property and he no longer has the debt. In that regard, it is the same as selling it for cash.

But the IRS does not look at it in this simple way. They must deal with everything in the abstract, and they have rules in Section 1031 for just this sort of thing.

The rule says that the assumption of the note by Baker is something being received by Adams in return for the property, and the "assumption" that is being received is "non-like kind" property to the property that Adams is purchasing as Replacement Property. That is, the assumption is not like kind to the real property. It is not like kind to the personal property. And it is not cash. Therefore, it is what is called "boot" paid to Adams. It is something received in addition to cash which has a fair market value. So it must be treated as boot. And boot is subject to taxation. But then, the rule says that the amount of boot received can be offset by the amount of new cash paid for the Replacement Property. In this case the amount of new cash being paid for the property will be $333,000.

So, (I've been waiting a long time to say this) the boot is moot.

But there is also a rule for situations where there is debt assumption involved in both transactions, the transaction involving the Relinquished Property and the transaction involving the Replacement Property.

That rule requires that the Exchangor "net the boot" if there is also boot involved in the purchase of the Replacement Property, and then assign the receipt of the positive amount to the party receiving it, who must then treat it as boot if doing a Section 1031 Exchange.

In this example, Adams received $18,000 of debt assumption in the first transaction, but he assumed $100,000 of debt in the second transaction. If we "net" the two amounts, Adams does not have a positive net amount of debt assumption received, because he received $18,000 worth of debt assumption and he provided $100,000 of debt assumption, so he does not have to report any boot. The $18,000 of debt assumed is treated the same as cash received and becomes part of the number that represents net cash received, which must be invested in the Replacement Property.

It also doesn't change the amount of capital gains, carryover of basis, new basis, nor the depreciation.

Smart investors do not get involved in debt assumptions. It is a pig's breakfast.

EXAMPLE #5 - SELLER FINANCING

Same as previous Examples, but when Adams sells his Duplex, Baker agrees to pay him $300,000 cash if he will take back a note for $100,000 in owner financing for ten years, then with a balloon payment of the principal balance remaining. The note will be payable to Adams.

What does this change?

RESULTS #5

We are again dealing with "boot."

When the Exchangor takes back a note from the Buyer, he is receiving property that is not like kind.

The property he is receiving is a promissory note. It is not like kind to real property, and it is not like kind to depreciable personal property, and it is not cash.

Therefore, the Exchangor is receiving boot, and the rules regarding boot will apply.

Boot is taxable up to the total amount received, or the gain on the transaction, whichever is less.

This entire $100,000 will be taxable to Adams because his capital gains is $228,244. If he had only made $50,000 on the sale instead of $228,244, then only $50,000 of the note amount would be taxable.

Of course, none of it will be taxable if Adams puts at least another $100,000 of his own money into the purchase of the Replacement Property. But let's look at what the situation would be if he did not.

The note represents a portion of his long term capital gains but since he will be receiving it monthly, it will not all be taxable at one time when he closes on the property, but rather as he receives it monthly. It will be reported under the Installment Sales provisions of Internal Revenue Code Section 453.

Each monthly payment will be part principal and part interest, as laid out on an Amortization Schedule, and will be reported on Form 1040, the interest reported on Schedule B and the capital gains reported on Schedule D.

The portion of the capital gains that will be taxed at the various marginal tax levels will be determined as you wind your way through filling out the forms.

In any event, it is not a good idea to have the note payable to the Exchangor.

We will cover that in the next Example.

EXAMPLE #6 - ALTERNATE SELLER FINANCING

Same as previous Example, but instead of the $100,000 note being made payable to Adams, it is made payable to the QI.

What does this change?

RESULTS #6

It simplifies a complicated problem.

When the note is made payable to the QI, the Exchangor is not in actual nor constructive receipt of it, and at the closing on the sale of the Relinquished Property, the note is sent to the QI, along with the rest of the net sales proceeds.

What the QI does with the note determines whether or not it eventually will become taxable to the Exchangor as boot.

The QI can do three things:

* sell the note to an investor, probably at a significant discount, and use the cash in the purchase of the Replacement Property,

* transfer the note to the Seller of the Replacement Property and it will be treated the same as cash, or

* sell the note, at full face value, to the Exchangor or a family member of the Exchangor, for cash, and use the cash in the purchase of the Replacement Property. The principal portion of each payment will then be tax-free to whoever buys it because it will be repayment on a debt, return of principal, and only the interest portion will be taxable.

A better alternative to all of these is to have the Exchangor require that the note be made payable in less than the 180-day time period for closing on the Replacement Property, and the QI will receive the money in time to use it as part of the purchase price.

If the QI is still holding the note when the closing on the Replacement Property takes place, he will endorse it over to the Exchangor, it will become taxable boot, and the Exchangor will treat it as an Installment Sale as described previously.

EXAMPLE #7 - BOOT

Same as Example #3, without debt assumption, and without seller financing, but when Adams sells the Relinquished Property, he receives a boat worth $40,000 and only $360,000 cash.

What effect does this have?

RESULTS #7

The Exchangor has received cash plus personal property in payment for the Relinquished Property, not "depreciable personal property" but "property owned by a person."

The cash is fine. It will go to the QI and be used to purchase the Replacement Property. The tax on it will be deferred.

But the personal property does not qualify for a Section 1031 Exchange because it is not property that Adams will hold "for productive use in a trade or business or for investment."

The boat will be considered boot and its value will be whatever cash price it would bring if sold on the open market. The buyer and seller can agree on this amount, and if it is not very much out of line, it will be acceptable to the IRS if ever questioned.

In this case the agreed-upon price is $40,000.

Adams has received the equivalent of $40,000 cash and this will be taxed as part of the capital gains that he has in the Duplex.

The bad part of this, as you probably already realize because we talked about it earlier, is that the IRS first collects the highest tax due among the bundle of incomes that represent the total capital gains amount, and in this case it would be the accelerated depreciation recapture at 39.6% of up to $15,200. The remaining $24,800 would be taxed at 25% as Unrecaptured Depreciation. Adams would pay $12,219 in taxes for receiving the boat.

Adams can only avoid this tax consequence if he adds an extra $40,000 to the net sales proceeds of the sale of the Relinquished Property when he purchases the Replacement Property. He cannot just add $40,000 to the new mortgage. He must actually add cash.

But if he has $40,000 cash available, a better plan would be to just buy the boat from Baker, and have Baker put that $40,000 with the other $360,000 and pay the full $400,000 in cash. That would avoid payment of the $12,219 in taxes.

There are a number of ways to deal with boot, but only one of them is good.

And that is to avoid it.

EXAMPLE #8 - NOT BOOT

Same as Example #3, but instead of borrowing $333,000 Adams only borrows $300,000 and includes a travel trailer that Carter is willing to accept at an agreed-upon value of $33,000.
How does this affect his Exchange?

RESULTS #8

There are three things that Adams must do to qualify for Section 1031 treatment when he purchases Replacement Property, in addition to making sure it is like kind.

* all of the net sales proceeds from the sale of the Relinquished Property must be used in the purchase of the Replacement Property,
* the value of the Replacement Property must be equal to, or greater than, the value of the Relinquished Property, and
* the Replacement Property must be "held either for productive use in a trade or business or for investment."

The fact that Adams includes personal property in the consideration he pays for the Replacement Property, in addition to all of the net sales proceeds, does not affect his Section 1031 Exchange.
It does not constitute boot in the same way that it would be considered boot if he were to be the one receiving it.
The only question is whether it would become part of the new consideration which would make up the depreciable basis of the Replacement Property.
The only consideration for Adams is to make sure that the

$33,000 agreed-upon value of the travel trailer is not more than his depreciable basis in the asset, if he has one, in which case he would have a capital gains liability just on the disposition of this item.

CONCLUSION

We have now covered all of the concepts involved in doing a Section 1031 Like Kind Exchange, with the preferred choice being a Delayed Exchange.

You should be able to take this knowledge and structure your own transaction.

But you should continue reading because there is much more information in the book, and it will only enhance the knowledge you have already acquired.

I will be covering the other two types of exchanges, the Reverse Exchange and the Construction Exchange, in the following Chapters.

Chapter 5

REVERSE EXCHANGE

OVERVIEW

A Reverse Exchange is the same as a Delayed Exchange, except that the Exchangor does things backwards. He purchases the Replacement Property before he sells the Relinquished Property. That's why it is called a Reverse Exchange.

The problem with a Reverse Exchange is that Section 1031 does not permit the Exchangor to own both properties at the same time, which he would if he bought his Replacement Property and still owned the property that is to become the Relinquished Property.

So, the IRS has provided a way to do it in Revenue Procedure 2000-37.

It requires the use of an entity called an Exchange Accommodation Titleholder (EAT) to hold either the Relinquished Property or the Replacement Property under a Qualified Exchange Accommodation Arrangement (QEAA) between the Exchangor and the Exchange Accommodation Titleholder (EAT).

What all of that means is that the Exchangor will sign an agreement with a QI that provides that the QI will set up a Limited Liability Company, usually referred to as an LLC, (a type of corporation) specifically for the purpose of being the EAT for the Exchangor. The QI will be the manager of the EAT and control it.

Then the Exchangor will sign a QEAA with the EAT.

The QEAA will state that:

* the intent is to do a Section 1031 Like Kind Exchange,

* the EAT is acquiring and holding the property solely for the benefit of the Exchangor in order to meet the 1031 requirements,

* the EAT will be considered the titleholder for income tax purposes, and

* the EAT will file the necessary tax returns and information reports.

Qualifications for an EAT are outlined in Treasury Regulation 1.1031(k)-1(k). But you will not have to do this yourself, your QI will do it (for a fee).

The situation can be handled in one of two ways:

* the EAT can purchase the Relinquished Property from the Exchangor and sell it, an arrangement we will call "Sell First," or

* the EAT can purchase the Replacement Property and hold it until the Exchangor has sold the Relinquished Property, and then sell the Replacement Property to the Exchangor, an arrangement we will call "Buy First."

SELL FIRST

In this scenario the Exchangor has found Replacement Property that he feels he must purchase immediately. He cannot wait until after he sells the Relinquished Property.

But he has three problems:

* he cannot hold title to both pieces of property at the same time, and

* he has not sold the Relinquished Property so he does not know the amount of net sales proceeds he will have to reinvest in the Replacement Property, and he needs that information in order to determine his down payment and note amount for the purchase of the Replacement Property, and

* he does not yet have the money to purchase the Replacement Property because he has not received his money from the sale of the Relinquished Property.

We will use Adams and his transaction as an example in analyzing this.

The first problem can be solved by transferring ownership of the Duplex, the "to-be" Relinquished Property, to the EAT under the terms of the QEAA. This is not considered a sale by Adams. He is just "parking" the Duplex out of his name. Then Adams can purchase the Replacement Property immediately.

When the EAT takes title to the Duplex, the EAT will assume any existing debt on the property, and sign a note for the remaining amount of the sales price, payable not to Adams, but to the QI, so that the QI can hold the net sales proceeds for Adams. The first time period has started running. The EAT will have 180 days from the date that it receives the Relinquished Property to transfer the Relinquished Property to a Buyer. If Adams already has a contract to sell the property that the EAT just took title to, the Duplex, he transfers that contract to the EAT. If he does not already have a contract, he will be responsible for finding a Buyer. When the EAT sells the property, the note that the EAT assumed will be paid off by the Title Company at Closing, from the sales proceeds, along with any other debts, and the EAT will instruct the Title Company to send the net funds to the QI. If Adams has not yet closed on the Replacement Property, the QI will notify the Title Company handling that transaction that the funds are available. If Adams has already closed on the purchase of the Replacement Property, the QI will send the funds to Adams, who will not be subject to taxation on the funds because he put the same amount of new money into the Replacement Property.

Also, remember, the EAT is just a "shell company." It has no office, no employees, etc., and the QI is the only member, the sole owner, and the manager. And the QI is not willing to manage the property that the EAT just acquired, during the period before the property can be sold. So, the terms of the QEAA can provide that the EAT leases the property back to Adams so that he can continue managing it without interruption.

The second problem of not knowing the exact amount of the net sales proceeds can be overcome by just making a good estimate. All of the numbers are known except for the eventual sales price, and Adams has projected a high, medium and low for that. Adams just picks the highest of his estimated sales prices, estimates his net sales proceeds, and he will still be safe if it is below that.

The third problem of not having the sales proceeds to purchase the Replacement Property will be discussed next.

BUY FIRST

This is the same scenario, the Exchangor has found Replacement Property that he wants to purchase immediately. He cannot wait until after he sells the Relinquished Property, and he does not want to give up the Relinquished Property first.

He has the same three problems:

* he cannot hold title to both pieces of property at the same time,

* he does not know the amount of net sales proceeds he will need to reinvest, and

* he does not have the money to purchase the Replacement Property because he does not have the proceeds from selling the Relinquished Property.

We will use Adams as an Example again.

The first problem of holding both pieces of property at the same time can be solved by use of the EAT.

Under the terms of the QEAA, the EAT will purchase the Replacement Property and hold it until Adams has sold the Relinquished Property. Then the EAT will sell the Replacement Property to Adams. The hold period requirement is 180 days.

The difficulty with the EAT purchasing the Replacement Property is that the EAT is an LLC that was set up by the QI and it is basically a paper entity. It has no assets, no business history, no credit, and no money. No lender will consider making a loan. And the QI will not be willing to borrow the money to buy the property. That is not their business model.

Adams might be able to find a bank to make a loan to the EAT and have the loan be guaranteed by Adams, but the property that is securing the loan will be owned by the LLC, not Adams, and the QI owns the LLC. The bank will probably not be comfortable with this, and the concept might even be against the banking regulations.

But let's assume that Adams is able to arrange a loan to the LLC and that loan will be secured by the property.

Adams still has to come up with the down payment, which would probably be at least 20% in order to qualify for the loan, but in this case will have to be much more.

Remember, in order to qualify for Section 1031 Exchange treatment, Adams must put into the Replacement Property all of the net sales proceeds from the sale of the Relinquished Property, which has not yet been sold.

But we can estimate what this will be. In fact, we already have.

If the sales price is $400,000 and the expenses of sale are $10,000 and the balance on the note of $18,000 is paid off, Adams will have net sales proceeds of $372,000.

This will have to be the amount of his down payment. He will have to loan this amount to the LLC and then arrange for the LLC to get a loan of $333,000 in order for the LLC, acting as the EAT, to purchase the Replacement Property for $705,000.

This seems highly unlikely to happen, but let's assume that it will, just so that we can see how the mechanics of a Reverse Exchange works.

1.) Adams signs or amends his contract with his QI containing all of the terms of their agreement regarding what the QI will be doing and how he will be doing it.

2.) The QI incorporates a legal entity called an LLC, and the QI is the sole member, owner, and manager. The LLC will act as the EAT.

3.) The QI drafts a QEAA for the EAT and Adams to sign.

4.) Adams loans $372,000 to the EAT with the note secured by all of the assets of the LLC and the note is payable on demand, and if no demand is made, in 180 days.

5.) Adams arranges with his bank to guarantee a loan to the EAT for $333,000 to be secured by the Replacement Property, and to be assumable by Adams if he either acquires the Replacement Property or acquires 100% ownership of the LLC.

6.) Adams signs a contract with the owner of the property to purchase the Fourplex for $700,000 and makes the contract assignable.

7.) Adams assigns the sales contract to the EAT.

8.) The EAT grants Adams an exclusive option to purchase the Replacement Property for $705,000, using the note owed to Adams by the EAT as an offsetting credit and agreeing to permit Adams to assume the bank loan.

9.) The EAT purchases the Replacement Property from Carl Carter, using the cash of $372,000 borrowed from Adams, and signing a note to the bank for $333,000. The EAT also signs an Assignment of Rents to the bank.

10.) The EAT leases the Replacement Property to Adams.

11.) Adams begins to manage the Replacement Property and begins making payments to the bank on the note from the rents collected.

12.) Adams identifies to his QI within 45 days three possible properties that he will sell as the Relinquished Property, one of them being, of course, the Duplex.

13.) Adams sells the Duplex as his Relinquished Property and the Title Company wires the funds to the QI.

14.) The EAT transfers title to the Replacement Property to Adams in return for cancellation of the $372,000 note and the assumption of the $333,000 bank note.

15.) The QI transfers the net sales proceeds of $372,000 received from the sale of the Relinquished Property to Adams, replacing the $372,000 that Adams loaned to the LLC.

16.) The QI files the necessary reports and tax returns, and then dissolves the LLC.

17.) Adams will report the 1031 Exchange on Form 8824 when he files his own tax return on April 15, 2018.

CONCLUSION

As you can see, the primary problem with doing a Reverse Exchange is the availability of money.

I have been asked why Adams would not just borrow the $372,000 that he needs for the down payment from the bank and put a second lien on the Duplex, and then when he sold the Duplex, the note could be paid off. That way, he would not have to use his own money.

The answer is that if the Relinquished Property is refinanced, and that's what he would be doing, within one year before it is sold, and that refinancing is tied to the circumstances of the 1031 Exchange, the IRS will consider this the same as receiving cash at the time of the sale, and the cash would be taxable. The refinancing would have the effect of reducing the amount of the "net sales proceeds" that Adams would be required to use to purchase the Replacement Property, and also have the effect of providing tax-free cash to Adams in the process, and the IRS considers this an attempt to circumvent the requirements of Section 1031.

Adams could have refinanced the property more than a year before the sale, but since he did not know that he would be needing the money, he would probably not have done that. Besides, there is a "lost opportunity" cost with just having money sitting in a bank earning no interest.

One technique that I have seen used by serious investors is to always have more than one investment property with significant equity. It is not easy to get into this position, but once you do, the opportunities are tremendous.

While Adams could not borrow the $372,000 that he needed by refinancing the property that would become the Relinquished Property, he could have borrowed it against the equity that he has in a warehouse that he owns. It would be a short-term loan, probably all due in six months, and probably would not cost him more than $12,000 in interest. If he could manage to get the entire Exchange done in 90 days, he could cut the cost to about $6,000. That is a reasonable expense for the use of $372,000 for three months. And it would allow him to do the deal.

Another observation that I would make about a Reverse Exchange involves the double payment of taxes.

Some states levy what is called a real estate transfer tax. That means that when you file a deed transferring real estate to a new owner, the local taxing authority assesses a fee of anywhere from $1.00 per $1,000 of valuation up to $8.00 per $1,000 of valuation.

That means that when the EAT files his deed after purchasing the Replacement Property, he could be taxed $5,600.

Then, shortly thereafter, when Adams files his deed from the EAT on the same property, he could have to pay $5,600.

This second fee could be avoided if, instead of the EAT deeding the property to Adams, the QI just transferred ownership of the LLC to Adams, since the LLC owns the property.

Now, immediately if you have been paying attention, you recognize that this is a problem because the name of the buyer of the Replacement Property would not be the same as the Seller of the Relinquished Property, as required by Section 1031.

But there is an anomaly in the law regarding LLCs that says that if the entity has only one member, that member can elect to have the LLC treated as what is called a "disregarded entity" and it is the same as the single member being the owner of the entity's assets, including those assets actually titled in recorded instruments in the name of the entity.

So Adams can actually receive his ownership in the Replacement Property by becoming the single-member owner of the LLC that owns the Replacement Property, and this would avoid the second payment of a real estate transfer tax, if he were faced with that problem where he lives.

And finally, you should be aware that in the world of Title Insurance, the rule is that the purchaser of the property receives a policy of title insurance that promises to reimburse him for any loss suffered by reason of a defect in title. But the policy only insures him, it does not insure any subsequent owners. If they want coverage, subsequent owners must purchase their own title policy. So, the EAT would be insured, but Adams would not.

However, there is also a provision in all state insurance laws that provides that if a purchaser is only acting as an accommodation titleholder, the Title Company can add an Endorsement to the Title Insurance Policy that also insures the person for whom the title is temporarily being held, in this case, Adams. But you have to ask for the Endorsement ahead of time.

As you can probably tell, I don't recommend that an individual attempt to do a Reverse Exchange. It is much more complex and somewhat more expensive than a Delayed Like Kind Exchange. But the decision is yours, and if you choose to go ahead, just make sure that you have a very good QI working with you. If you survive it, you will become a stronger investor.

Of course, property developers and investment companies should have no hesitation using this technique. You probably have the manpower and financial resources to handle it, and sometimes it is just necessary to do it this way for a variety of reasons.

Author's Note:

Construction Exchanges are becoming very popular with real estate investors who want to build a portfolio of income properties that they buy from wholesalers and rehab and hold. If you can master this (somewhat) complicated process within the Section 1031 framework, you will have a major advantage over your competition.

Chapter 6

CONSTRUCTION EXCHANGE

OVERVIEW

A Construction Exchange is the same as a Delayed Exchange, but a Construction Exchange also includes the use of an Exchange Accommodation Titleholder (EAT) like a Reverse Exchange, because, in this case, the Replacement Property does not yet exist. The land is there, but the building has not yet been built.

Therefore, a Construction Exchange must be handled like a Reverse Exchange, because the Replacement Property will be constructed over time, and title to the property will be held by the EAT while the construction is being done during the exchange period, and then transferred to the Exchangor.

For our example, assume that Adams wants to sell his Duplex because it is in a part of town where the growth has leveled out. And instead of buying a Fourplex as the Replacement Property, he wants to build a Fourplex in a part of town near a new office complex and a trade school, where he has found an ideal lot, and where there are no other Fourplexes in the area.

The rules of the Delayed Exchange and the Reverse Exchange apply, so we won't repeat them.

The difference here is that the Fourplex has not been built, and Adams will have to build it, or have it built, because if he sells his Duplex and buys the lot, the Exchange is over at that point, the lot is considered the Replacement Property, and whatever amount of the net sales proceeds from the closing on the Relinquished Property is not spent on the lot will be distributed to him and will be taxable, which would be huge.

The only way he can do this is to not take title to the lot, but still build the Fourplex on the lot, which he does not own.

This will require the use of an Exchange Accommodation Titleholder (EAT) which will take title to the property and hold it until the Fourplex can be built on it and then sell it to Adams.

Of course, this is not the only way that a Construction Exchange can be done. There have been many other methods suggested for doing a Construction Exchange, but you should be very careful in considering any of them.

One such method is for Adams to lease the property from the owner under a "Lease and Build" agreement, and then buy it when it is finished. This is probably workable, but involves a lot of questions. Because Adams is doing the construction, does he already own the building he constructed on the lot, the leasehold improvements, at the time of closing, and therefore is only buying the lot when he closes on the property? The answer would depend on the real estate law of the state where the construction takes place. But remember, the IRS does not have to follow state law regarding real property ownership and transfer. The IRS can characterize any transaction any way they please for tax purposes. Also, it is just never a good idea to build on real estate owned by someone else. What about judgments, liens, bankruptcy, foreclosure, divorce, mental incompetency, and various other possible complications involving the property owner? The bank is looking to you for their money, and you have their money tied up in property built on a lot that is in someone else's name.

So, while "Lease and Build" agreements are viable under some circumstances, they might not be appropriate in this case.

Another suggestion has been to put the property into the name of the contractor and sign a purchase agreement with him and pay him as he builds. I don't see a smart investor ever doing something like that. Many contractors are great people, but what about the others?

So we are back to our original plan. Adams will first sign his contract with the Qualified Intermediary (QI) and agree on what is to be done, and how it is to be done.

Then the QI will draft the Qualified Exchange Accommodation Agreement (QEAA) for Adams to sign, and it will provide for the QI to set up a Limited Liability Company (LLC) to act as the EAT.

Now Adams will get busy with lining up the purchase of the land and arranging the sale of his Relinquished Property.

RELINQUISHED PROPERTY

Adams will first arrange for the sale of his Duplex, and provide in the sales contract that the closing will take place within 30 days, with an option for him to extend the time for another 30-day period, giving him the flexibility he needs.

For this Example we will use approximately the same information that we used in "Example #3 - A Typical Transaction" in Chapter 4 on Delayed Exchange.

* Adams bought a Duplex ten years ago for $200,000.
* The price was allocated $20,000 land and $180,000 building.
* The furnishings were of negligible value, none assigned.

* He put the building on his Depreciation Schedule at $180,000 for 27.5 years.

* He has taken $65,400 straight-line depreciation on the building.

* He spent $30,000 capital improvements on two garages.

* He borrowed the $30,000 from the bank, put a lien on the property.

* The balance of the note is now $18,000.

* He has taken $7,644 straight-line depreciation on the garages.

* He spent $20,000 cash on new furniture and furnishings.

* He has taken $15,200 accelerated depreciation on them.

* His capital improvements total is $50,000 ($30,000 + $20,000).

* His total depreciation is $88,244 ($65,400 + $7,644 + $15,200).

* His basis in the property is $161,756 ($200,000 + $50,000 - $88,244).

* Bob Baker, the Buyer, has offered him $400,000 for the Duplex.

* His total costs of the sale will be the $10,000 closing costs.

* His net sales proceeds will be $372,000 ($400,000 - 10,000 - 18,000).

* His capital gains will be $228,244 ($400,000 - $10,000 - $161,756).

REPLACEMENT PROPERTY

Adams will negotiate the contract to buy the vacant lot for $70,000 and make sure that the contract can be assigned. He will deliver the contract to the Title Company, along with an Earnest Money Deposit check, payable to the Title Company, and instruct the Title Company to hold the check because it will be replaced by the entity to which the contract will be assigned. Note, however, that some title companies operate under state regulations that require them to deposit earnest money checks into their escrow account within three working days of receipt. If you run into this situation, just put language in the sales contract that the earnest money check must be delivered within thirty days, and the check can be provided by the EAT after the contract is assigned to that entity, as described later.

Adams will become the General Contractor. He will take his building plans and construction schedule to various sub-contractors and get bids on the work to be done.

Adams will also take his building plans to various building supply companies and have them compile a list of materials and give him a bid on supplying the necessary items.

The QI will form the Limited Liability Company (LLC) that will act as the Exchange Accommodation Titleholder (EAT).

Adams will identify to his QI the Replacement Property to be built. He will use the street address, the lot and block number, and the legal description of the land. For the construction, he will describe the Fourplex by total square footage, the total square footage of each unit, and a description of each unit as to number of bedrooms and bathrooms, and might even attach a copy of his building plans. He can make changes up until 180 days after the Exchange Date, which will be the date on which the EAT closes on the purchase of the lot.

Adams will assign his contract for the purchase of the land to the EAT.

Adams will arrange a loan from his bank to the EAT for $700,000 to be used to purchase the land for $70,000 plus closing costs, and build the Fourplex for actual costs up to $630,000, with the loan guaranteed by Adams, and assumable by Adams, but secured by the lot and the construction. Loan payments will begin after 180 days. He will provide the bank a copy of his building plans, the tax appraisal on the land, the bids on the building materials, and a To-Be-Built Appraisal prepared by a Certified Appraiser. Adams and the bank will agree on a Draw Schedule for the loan funds.

The EAT will purchase the land. The date on which this occurs becomes the Exchange Date. Within 45 days Adams must identify to his QI three possible properties that will become the Relinquished Property. Within 180 days, Adams must take title to the Replacement Property from the EAT.

If Adams did not provide an Earnest Money Check to the Title Company, the EAT will do so. If he did provide a check, the EAT will replace the Earnest Money Check at the Title Company with a new check, using funds from the loan, and instruct the Title Company to return the first check to Adams, or a refund check.

The EAT will sign a Lease And Development contract with Adams for Adams to lease the land and complete the construction with funds provided by the bank. The bank will sign the contract pro forma, indicating awareness and agreement.

Adams will hire a Construction Manager to supervise the subcontractors, scheduling and inspecting their work, and replacing any of them when necessary.

Adams will close on the sale of his Duplex and the net sales proceeds will be sent to his QI who will hold them until Adams closes on the purchase of the Replacement Property. It will not be necessary for Adams to identify the Relinquished Property to his QI because the sale has taken place within the 45-day identification period.

Adams will proceed with preparing the land for construction, subbing in the utilities, and pouring the foundation.

Adams will then proceed through the construction process in an orderly manner. Any sub-contractor who is not available when he is scheduled to begin work or does not proceed efficiently with his work is replaced by another sub-contractor.

Adams will either complete the construction before the expiration of the 180-day period, or he will not.

Either way, Adams will still have a valid 1031 Exchange, but with different numbers.

We will look at it both ways.

CONSTRUCTION IS COMPLETE

Adams is able to complete the construction within the 180-day period from the time that the EAT purchased the land.

We will assume that the entire $700,000 of the bank loan funds were used.

The QI will arrange for the sale of the Replacement Property by the EAT to Adams.

The QI will transfer to the Title Company the $372,000 net sales proceeds from the sale of the Relinquished Property, which the Title Company will use to pay down the $700,000 bank loan.

Adams will sign an Assumption of the bank loan with a balance of $328,000.

Adams now owns a $700,000 new Fourplex.

His tax deferred capital gains in the Replacement Property is $228,244.

The actual capital gains portion of this is $140,000.

The straight-line depreciation portion subject to 25% recapture tax is $73,044.

The accelerated depreciation portion subject to 39.6% recapture tax is $15,200.

His carryover basis in the property is $161,756 ($200,000 + $50,000 - $88,244).

The amount of new money or new debt put into the property is $328,000.

He paid $70,000 for the land, leaving $630,000 paid for the building. Of this amount, $228,244 represents the capital gains from the sale of the Relinquished Property and $161,756 represents the basis of the Relinquished Property transferred into the Replacement Property.

Therefore his basis in the Replacement Property is $300,000 ($700,000 - 228,244 - 161,756). Add this to the basis of $161,756 transferred in and he has a new basis in the Replacement Property of $461,756. Subtract the $70,000 for the land, and his depreciable basis in the Replacement Property is $391,756.

CONSTRUCTION IS NOT COMPLETE

Although everyone extended their best efforts, Adams was not able to complete the construction by the end of the 180-day period. He recognized after 160 days that this was going to happen. So, he scheduled closing on the purchase of the Replacement Property from the EAT in its unfinished condition.

His first task was to total up all of the money that had been spent on the project at that point. It came to $180,000 spent on materials and $140,000 on labor, including $10,000 paid thus far to the Construction Manager. The total was $320,000. But $20,000 of the materials were appliances that had been delivered but were not ready to be installed because the flooring and the interior painting had not been done. So the total amount that he could count was $300,000. He can't count everything that has been delivered to the site, only what has become part of the construction.

Another $70,000 had been spent for the land, so the total that had gone into the property at this point was $370,000.

But the net sales proceeds from the sale of the Relinquished Property was $372,000.

That means that if he closes on the Replacement Property at this point, the exchange will not qualify for total tax deferral because the value of $370,000 is not equal to, or greater than, the net sales proceeds of $372,000. So all of the net sales proceeds would not have been put into the Replacement Property.

Adams has 20 days before closing, so he hooks up all of the appliances so that he can add that $20,000 to the total, and he brings in the painters to do enough of the painting to add another $10,000 to the total.

He closes before the 180-day deadline and the total value of the Replacement Property at that point is $400,000 so he has satisfied the requirement that it be equal to, or greater than, the Relinquished Property and that all of the net sales proceeds be put into the Replacement Property.

He has also satisfied an unwritten requirement of the IRS for "substantial completion" of the construction in order to close on the property. The Regulations provide no percentage, ratio, or fraction to be used as a guideline, but it is a good idea to be past the halfway point and beyond the dry-in stage, with all permits in place and utilities ready to hook up.

When Adams closes on the Fourplex, the QI transfers the $372,000 net sales proceeds being held from the sale of the Relinquished Property to the Title Company, which uses it to pay down the bank loan from $700,000 to $328,000, and Adams still has $300,000 of the loan that has not been drawn on, since only $400,000 has been used.

Adams completes the Fourplex during the next two months and only uses $250,000 of the available loan funds.

He now has a new Fourplex that cost $650,000.

He has tax deferred capital gains in the Replacement Property of $228,244.

The actual capital gains portion of this is $140,000.

The straight-line depreciation portion subject to 25% recapture tax is $73,044.

The accelerated depreciation portion subject to 39.6% recapture tax is $15,200.

His carryover basis in the property is $161,756 ($200,000 + $50,000 - $88,244).

The amount of new money or new debt put into the property is $278,000.

He paid $70,000 for the land, leaving $580,000 for the building.

Subtracting the $228,244 of capital gains transferred into the new property, we have $351,756 in depreciable basis in the new property.

CONCLUSION

A regular Delayed Exchange can be done by a busy real estate investor who is mostly a passive investor. If you find a competent QI, it will be monitoring the entire process.

A Reverse Exchange will require quite a bit more time. But, again, with a good QI helping you handle it, it can be done by an individual with good organization and attention to detail.

But anyone doing a Construction Exchange should probably be ready to spend pretty much every day with the process, and have the assistance of at least one experienced building professional.

Turning it over to other people and expecting them to show up and perform is a train wreck waiting to happen. And the stakes are too high. If you cannot devote virtually full time and handle this yourself, you probably should not do it.

Remember to register for free updates at:
www.S1031Exchange.com

Chapter 7

FORM 8824

REPORTING REQUIREMENTS

At the end of the year in which you began your 1031 Exchange, you will be required to report the Exchange on your tax return, even in cases where the Exchange is not completed until the following year. If your Exchange is not completed by the April 15 deadline for reporting it, you should get an extension on your filling deadline.

Your tax return will be a Form 1040 if you are an individual.

Failure to report the Exchange will invalidate your Exchange, and trigger the capital gains tax and the depreciation recapture.

The form used to report the Exchange is Form 8824, Like-Kind Exchanges, and you will attach it to your Form 1040. The Form is divided into Part I through Part IV, but Part II concerns transactions with Related Parties and Part IV concerns transactions by certain government officials with conflicts of interest, so you will only be concerned with Part I and Part III for a regular transaction.

It might help you to see what we are working with. You can view and download the Form at irs.gov/pub/irs-pdf/f8824.pdf.

The Instructions are at irs.gov/pub/irs-pdf/i8824.pdf.

The IRS does not have a Publication which explains Like Kind Exchanges, like it does for other transactions.

First, let's discuss where you will get the information that will be required to complete the form.

When you close on each of your properties, sale of the Relinquished Property and purchase of the Replacement Property, you will receive a HUD-1 Settlement Statement to inspect and approve, and then you will be asked to sign it. You will take a copy with you when you leave the closing. This document is protected by the laws of confidentiality, and will not be given to anyone else, so take care of your copy.

HUD-1 SETTLEMENT STATEMENT

Some of the items on your HUD-1 Settlement Statement might be marked with the symbol "POC" and that means "Paid outside closing." For instance, the Surveyor might have required payment before releasing the survey, and you might have paid for that. If so, the amount that you paid will be shown, probably on line 1301 of page 2, and will be marked "Survey POC" and show the amount that was paid.

Otherwise, all of the important information related to your transaction, and most of what you need to complete Form 8824, will be identified and reported on the HUD-1.

* Name of Buyer,
* Name of Seller,
* Property location,
* Settlement date,
* Contract sales price,
* Value assigned to personal property,
* Loan payoff amount,
* Deposit or earnest money,

* Amount of new loan,
* Existing loan assumed,
* Amount of real estate commission,
* Amount of property taxes,
* Reserves deposited with the lender,
* Charges for the closing and title insurance, and
* Recording fees for documents.

PART I

This section of Form 8824 is called "Information on the Like-Kind Exchange" and contains seven lines requesting information about your Exchange.

* Line 1. Description of like-kind property given up.
Insert a brief description such as "Duplex located at 123 Anywhere Street, City, State, Zip." If the transaction involved personal property, add something like "Furniture, furnishings, and appliances for six bedrooms, two living rooms, two laundry rooms, two kitchens, and four bathrooms."
Don't worry about whether you are providing enough information. If you are not, and the IRS wants more, they will just ask you. You will not suffer any consequences. Just make sure that the information you do provide is accurate.

* Line 2. Description of like-kind property received.
Enter information similar to the above for the Replacement Property.

* Line 3. Date like-kind property given up was originally acquired.

This is asking for the date you acquired the Relinquished Property. This will prove that your capital gains is actually long-term.

* Line 4. Date you actually transferred your property to the other party.

This will be a date more than 12 months from the date in the line above. For a regular Delayed Exchange this will be your Exchange Date. For a Reverse Exchange or a Construction Exchange, it will be a different date. See Chapter 5 and Chapter 6 to determine that date.

* Line 5. Date like-kind property you received was identified by written note to another party.

This is the date you notified your QI under the 45-day period. If you received your Replacement Property prior to the 45-day period and did no notification, enter the date that you received the Replacement Property.

* Line 6. Date you actually received the like-kind property from other party.

This is the date that you closed on your Replacement Property and will show that you satisfied the 180-day period.

* Line 7. Was the exchange of the property given up or received made with a related party, either directly or indirectly. If "Yes," complete Part II. If "No," go to Part III.

We are assuming that you have not done an Exchange with a Related Party, so you will mark this "No" and go on to Part III.

If you need help with any of this information, you should ask your QI.

PART III

This section is called "Realized Gain or (Loss), Recognized Gain, and Basis of Like-Kind Property Received."
It contains lines 12 through 25.

Lines 12 through 14 are used to report any part of your Relinquished Property transaction which was not like kind property. On line 12 you report the fair market value of that property and on line 13 you report your basis in the property, then subtract line 13 from line 12, and put the results on line 14.
Skip lines 12 through 14 if all of the Relinquished Property was like kind, which we are assuming that it is.

* Line 15. Cash received, FMV of other property received, plus net liabilities assumed by other party, reduced (but not below zero) by any exchange expenses you incurred.
This is the way the IRS asks if you received any boot. For Adams this number is zero.

* Line 16. FMV of like-kind property you received.
This is the sales price of your Replacement Property plus any cost of acquisition. For Adams this number is $705,000.

* Line 17. Add lines 15 and 16.
You can do this. It is $705,000.

* Line 18. Adjusted basis in like-kind property you gave up, net amounts paid to other party, plus any exchange expenses not used on line 15.
The adjusted basis in the Duplex is $161,756. The bank loan was $333,000. The total is $494,789, but remember that we have

to subtract the amount of $18,000 as the loan payoff amount, and the total for this line is $476,756.

* Line 19. Realized gain or (loss). Subtract line 18 from line 17.
This number is $228,244. This is the amount of capital gains to be deferred.

* Line 20. Enter the smaller of line 15 or line 19.
This number is zero.

* Line 21. Ordinary income under recapture rules. Enter here and on Form 4797, line 16.
If this had not been a tax deferred exchange, but only a partially deferred exchange, some of the gain would have been taxable, and if that part had been the recapture of depreciation at the ordinary income tax rate, it would be entered here. The number is zero.

* Line 22. Subtract line 21 from line 20.
Zero from zero is zero.

* Line 23. Recognized gain. Add lines 21 and 22.
This is how much of the capital gains is being taxed instead of being tax deferred. Zero plus zero is zero.

* Line 24. Deferred gain or (loss). Subtract line 23 from 19.
This shows how much of the capital gains is being carried over with tax deferral. It is the entire amount shown on line 19, $228,244.

* Line 25. Basis of like-kind property received. Subtract line 15 from the sum of lines 18 and 23.

This is the depreciable basis in Adams new Fourplex. The amount is $476,756. If you will notice, you add this to the amount of deferred capital gains of $228,244 and you get the total of $705,000, the amount paid for the Fourplex. You can also get $705,000 by adding the net sales proceeds of $372,000 to the bank loan of $333,000.

CONCLUSION

Form 8824 is a very difficult form to complete.

The IRS starts by assuming that two parties are swapping two pieces of property, which never happens. They also assume that each party is assuming the other party's debt, which never happens. They also assume that one party is receiving the other party's property, plus some money, which almost never happens. The form uses phrases like "like-kind property you gave up" and "net amounts paid to other party" and "FMV of other property received," without any explanation of what they mean by "gave up" or "other party" or "other property" or what numbers you are supposed to "net" so that you can figure the amount.

In the Instructions, they try to explain things by using an example, which is one that I have never seen anything similar to in thirty years of handling thousands of real estate closings.

But don't be intimidated by the Form. Understand your transaction and figure out what your numbers are supposed to be, and then make them fit where you know they are supposed to go, and assume that is what they are asking for.

Your QI can be a great help in dealing with this situation.

Author's Note:

Please be careful. Real estate investors are being advised that they can do a Section 1031 Like Kind Exchange, and then get all of their net sales proceeds from the first sale back into their pocket by immediately refinancing the Replacement Property. This is not true. Why would the IRS require that all net sales proceeds from the sale of the Relinquished Property be used to purchase the Replacement Property, and then allow you to get it back out fifteen minutes later by adding new debt? If this were OK, they would just allow you to use debt instead of the net sales proceeds in the first place. Again, be very wary of anyone giving you this advice.

Chapter 8

CREATIVE FINANCING

OVERVIEW

Let's talk about money.

Everything about Section 1031 revolves around money, the good and the bad.

The good is that you are saving it by not paying the taxes.

The bad is that you must put everything you get from selling the Relinquished Property into the Replacement Property.

But there might be an alternate set of circumstances under which you do not lose forever the use of your net sales proceeds.

AN ALTERNATE PLAN

There is actually a way that you can avoid paying taxes on the capital gains that you have built up in your property over the years without doing a Section 1031 Like Kind Exchange, and still use that capital gains to buy another property, just like you would buy the Replacement Property in a Section 1031 Exchange.

And the best part is that you keep the property that you would have sold as your Relinquished Property, ending up with both properties, and you save the time and money that you would spend doing a Section 1031 Exchange.

By refinancing your existing property, you can free up your equity and use it to buy another property. The proceeds of the loan are not taxable so the transaction does not have to be reported to the IRS.

In the scenario that we are using involving Adams, instead of selling his Duplex for $400,000 and being forced to use all of his money from the sale (his net sales proceeds) to put into the new property, he can refinance the Duplex. He has paid down the note on the property to about $20,000 and he has a good credit history with his lender, so he should be treated as a very valuable customer.

He will need an appraisal showing the fair market value of the Duplex to be $400,000 and he will need to show three years of income statements on the property proving that there is sufficient cash flow to service the loan. In fact, he might request that the Appraiser do an appraisal based on "income production" instead of the usual method of "comparable properties" and end up with an even higher appraised value.

If his credit rating is acceptable, any bank would be willing to loan him 80% of the appraised value, but his current lender would probably be his best choice. This would be a loan of $320,000. After paying off the balance of approximately $20,000 on the existing note, he is left with $300,000 to invest any way he wants. And the best part is that he still owns the property, and it is cash-flowing and going up in value.

Banks are accustomed to doing this and they are familiar with how the process works. Most serious investors borrow against the equity in their properties.

Adams could split the $300,000 loan proceeds into two $150,000 down payments of 20%, and get two bank loans of $600,000 representing the other 80%, and he will have the funds to buy two Fourplexes at $750,000 each.

And he would still own his $400,000 Duplex in addition to the two new properties.

ANOTHER ALTERNATE PLAN

It is also possible to combine refinancing with a Section 1031 Like Kind Exchange.

You can refinance your Relinquished Property before you sell it in the 1031 Exchange, and you can refinance your Replacement Property after you have completed your 1031 Exchange.

But there are rules.

REFINANCE RELINQUISHED PROPERTY

This plan involves taking equity out of your Relinquished Property before doing the Exchange so that you only have to put the smallest amount necessary into the Replacement Property.

There is quite a bit of confusion among real estate investors concerning this aspect of the Section 1031 Like Kind Exchange process. There are even some self-declared authorities claiming that an investment property does not qualify for a Section 1031 Exchange if it has been recently refinanced. This is complete nonsense.

Section 1031(a) requires that the Relinquished Property be held for productive use in a trade or business or held for investment. The remainder of the language in Section 1031 says absolutely nothing about the amount of debt on the property or when the debt was created.

Let's look at our Example. Adams will sell his Duplex for $400,000 and pay $10,000 closing cost, netting $390,000 and then pay off the approximately $20,000 balance on the mortgage, winding up with $370,000 net sales proceeds.

He must use all of the $370,000 net sales proceeds in the purchase of his Replacement Property in order to qualify for tax deferral under Section 1031.

But what if he refinanced his Duplex by borrowing $250,000? After paying off the $20,000 balance on the mortgage, he would have $230,000 in an investment account to do with what he pleased.

Then when he sold the Duplex for $400,000 and netted $390,000 he would be paying off a $250,000 mortgage and only have $140,000 net sales proceeds that he would have to use in the purchase of his Replacement Property.

The $140,000 would still be enough of a down payment to qualify him for an 80% loan of $560,000 so that he could buy the Fourplex for $700,000 as his Replacement Property. He still qualifies for the tax deferral of Section 1031 and ends up with an extra $230,000 cash in an investment account. He can use that as a down payment to qualify for another 80% loan of $920,000 and end up purchasing another income property for $1,150,000 in addition to his $700,000 Fourplex.

It's all about leverage. But, more importantly, it's about timing.

If you refinance your Relinquished Property within a year before the Exchange Date, the date that you sell the property, the IRS could argue that this is the same as cashing out, and as an attempt to avoid the rules for qualifying for a Section 1031 Exchange. The IRS might also re-characterize the loan proceeds as capital gains income.

There is no provision in the Internal Revenue Code or in the Treasury Regulations that provides more guidance on this, but we know that the "lookback" period is at least one year, and might even be two tax-years, meaning two "December-31-year-ends."

But in all cases, the IRS looks at your intent, and at the surrounding business environment and your particular circumstances.

If you come across a great investment opportunity, and can only take advantage of it by accessing the equity in your investment property, and you do a refinance, you cannot be punished for doing so.

And if, two months later, you find the Fourplex you have been looking for, and you make a business decision to sell that refinanced investment property and do a Section 1031 Like Kind Exchange, your Exchange will qualify for Section 1031 treatment.

You should discuss this with your QI and with a knowledgeable tax professional before you make the decision.

REFINANCE REPLACEMENT PROPERTY

There are also no Internal Revenue Code or Treasury Regulations guidelines for refinancing the Replacement Property after you have acquired it.

The answer about when you can do it depends on your particular circumstances.

But in general, the IRS will not be concerned if you refinance your Replacement Property within a reasonable time period after you acquire it, and the decision has "some business substance."

Even a month later, you could get an 80% loan that would, in effect, allow you to take out all of the capital gains from the sale of your Relinquished Property that you were forced to put into the Replacement Property, and use that as a down payment on another investment property.

In the case of Adams, he has ended up with a $705,000

piece of property as his Replacement Property and he put a mortgage of $333,000 on it. But if he were to get an 80% loan on the property, that would be $564,000 and after paying off the $333,000 it would leave him with $231,000 to use for other investment purposes.

The results are similar to what would happen if he refinanced the Relinquished Property, as described above.

But this is a risky area, and doing it only one month after closing could be seen as an attempt to circumvent the provisions of Section 1031.

The safe route is to do the refinancing for a legitimate business purpose which did not exist, and could not have been foreseen, before the closing, but came up at that particular time, no other financing alternative was available to you, and therefore the refinancing was "in the normal course of business."

But this would be a very hard sell to the IRS. Chances of success: probably less than 20%.

All circumstances are different, and you should always get a legal opinion from your attorney, or whoever your trusted professional advisor is, before you embark on this path.

Chapter 9

DEPRECIATION AND RECAPTURE

SECTION 1250 PROPERTY

The IRS divides assets into different types and categories for easy reference.

The two types that we are concerned about are referred to as Section 1250 property and Section 1245 property.

The first category, Section 1250 property, is the depreciable real estate that makes up the buildings and attached fixtures in our businesses and investments.

This property is depreciated in a straight-line method over the IRS-mandated 27.5 years of its productive life for residential rental units, and 39 years for commercial property, regardless of how new or old it is. "Straight-line method" means that an equal amount of depreciation allowance is deducted as an expense each year until the entire price of the property is taken as depreciation.

When Adams originally bought his Duplex he put it on his Depreciation Schedule with a life of 27.5 years and a basis of $180,000. Remember that he paid $200,000 for the property, but assigned a value of $20,000 to the land, which is not depreciable. He depreciated the Duplex for ten years, or 120 months, and took $545 per month in depreciation allowance, or a total of $6,540 per year, which is a total for the ten-year period of $65,400.

He has reduced his basis in the Duplex to $114,600. When you see the term "depreciated basis" or "book value" in reference to an asset, this is the number, plus the land value, that is being referred to.

Adams also did $30,000 worth of capital improvements three years after he bought the Duplex by building two garages, and he put the capital improvements on his Depreciation Schedule with the straight-line method for 27.5 years, and took $91 per month in depreciation allowance, or a total of $1,092 per year, and had a seven-year total of $7,644.

This reduced his basis in the "Capital Improvements - Duplex," which is how his two garages are identified on his forms, from $30,000 to $22,356.

His total straight-line depreciation taken on the building plus the capital improvements is $73,044.

SECTION 1245 PROPERTY

The property that we are concerned about that fits into the category of Section 1245 property is everything in our package of business assets that is not real estate. This will be things like the furniture and furnishings in a rent house or Duplex, or the furnishings and equipment in the laundry room of an apartment building, and so forth.

Usually, this is property on which you will claim a depreciation allowance as a deduction from income, because the property was used by you in the business that produced the income. The

IRS refers to it as "personal property" but don't be confused, it is part of your business package. They know it is being used in a business, they just mean that it is not real estate, therefore it is "personal" under their terminology. This is how the IRS looks at it.

When Adams bought his Duplex, it included both Section 1250 and Section 1245 property. But the Section 1245 property was of very low value because it was old used furniture. So he did not assign a value to it and, instead, chose to include everything as Section 1250 property and depreciate the entire $180,000 amount that way.

The IRS allows this to be done under certain circumstances.

If the total value of the Section 1245 property is not more than 15% of the total value of the Section 1245 and Section 1250 property together (not including the land), you can do this. However, you will lose valuable depreciation deductions if you do this, as I have explained in earlier chapters.

When Adams started to think about selling his Duplex two years ago, he decided to upgrade it so that he could raise the rents, and he spent $20,000 on new furniture and furnishings.

This is the type of property that comes under the definition of Section 1245.

Section 1245 property does not have to be depreciated over a 27.5 year period.

The IRS has a very complicated method of classifying Section 1245 depreciable assets, and assigning a useful life to them, and it is more than what we can go into here.

But basically, the taxpayer can choose to use one of four methods.

* straight-line,
* 150% declining balance,
* 200% declining balance, or
* sum-of-the-years digits

Most taxpayers choose the 200% declining balance method, also called Double Declining Balance, and referred to as DDB, because it provides the largest depreciation deduction from income each year.

The IRS also allows the taxpayer to claim a Section 179 bonus deduction for the first year that the assets, if they are new, are placed in service, and the bonus amount can be up to 50% of the cost. You might elect this option in order to boost your depreciation deduction if you need or want it in the first year, or you might decline it if you think you will need the depreciation deductions more in later years.

Adams was required to list the furniture and furnishings in an asset depreciation category called "Furniture & Equipment."

He was required to assign it a sub-category called "5-year Residential rental furnishings."

He chose to take the Section 179 bonus depreciation of $10,000 the first year.

He also claimed $2,000 the first year using what is called the "Half-year convention" and claimed $3,200 the second year under the DDB method.

His total claimed depreciation of the Section 1245 property is $15,200.

His depreciated basis in the property is $4,800.

DEPRECIATION RECAPTURE

Section 1250

As you know, when you sell a capital asset, and you make a profit, you will pay capital gains tax on the profit.

The capital gains tax is either 0% or 15% or 20%, depending on your marginal tax bracket. For simplicity, we are assuming a 20% capital gains tax bracket.

Adams purchased a capital asset, a Duplex, for $200,000 and assigned $20,000 value to the land, leaving $180,000 for the building, and he claimed $65,400 of straight-line depreciation, leaving him with a depreciated basis in the building of $114,600 and $20,000 in the land.

He added $30,000 in capital improvements and claimed $7,644 of straight-line depreciation, leaving him with a depreciated basis in the capital improvements of $22,356.

His total depreciated basis in the property and improvements is $156,956.

The total straight-line depreciated claimed is $73,044.

If you notice, the total of these two numbers is $230,000.

In other words, his depreciated basis in the property is the purchase price plus improvements less the depreciation taken.

Adams plans to sell the property for $400,000.

But he will sell the furniture and furnishings separately for $4,800, which I have described earlier and which I will explain in the next section, so his actual sales price for the building and improvements will be $395,200 less $10,000 sales cost, leaving $385,200.

Remember we are only talking about the real estate here.

His capital gains will be the sales price of $385,200 less his basis of $156,956.

This is $228,244 in capital gains.

Part of this capital gains is due to the property actually increasing in fair market value from $230,000 to $385,200, a total of $155,200.

And part of this capital gains is due to the basis in the property going down from $230,000 to $156,956 because of the $73,044 of depreciation that was taken.

Adams will pay 20% capital gains tax on $155,200, the portion of his $228,234 capital gains that was caused by the increase in market value from what he paid for it to what he sold it for.

But the other $73,044 of the capital gains that was created because of the depreciation taken, lowering his basis, will be taxed at a different tax rate.

This is called "depreciation recapture" and it is taxed at a maximum rate of 25%. If you are in the 10% or 15% marginal income tax bracket, you are only taxed at 15%, not 25%.

On his tax return, if Adams were not doing a Section 1031 Exchange, he would report the sale on his Schedule D, and separately identify this portion of his capital gains as "Unrecaptured Section 1250 Gain" and the IRS will know to pull it out and tax it at the higher rate.

Section 1245

As noted above, this type of property is usually depreciated at an accelerated rate and even receives bonus depreciation if it is new when placed in service.

The IRS rule for accelerated depreciation is that, when it is recaptured, it will be taxed at the ordinary tax rate of the individual taxpayer, in other words, up to 39.6%.

Their logic behind this, although debatable, is that since the business income would have been taxed at ordinary income rates, and since this depreciation reduced the amount of ordinary income that was subjected to taxes, when this depreciation is recaptured, the recapture just represents delayed taxation of what would have been ordinary income.

The concept seems to ignore the fact that you spent your own money to purchase the asset that was being depreciated in the first place, money which the IRS was allowing you to recover over an extended period of time, but which now they will tax you on.

In other words, they are taxing you on money which you spent to purchase an asset to use in your business. Not money you earned, money you spent.

But if you go back far enough, you will see that the original concept for putting assets into the business was that they would be used up in the production of income. In other words, their value would eventually go to zero, so the money paid for them should be deducted over time as the income is being produced.

But if the assets do not decrease in value to zero, and might even go up in value, such as the Duplex, then the depreciation that was taken should be "recaptured" and taxed as income.

So the position of the IRS is actually reasonable.

And that brings us to the primary difference between Section 1250 property such as buildings, which usually does go up in value, and where the depreciation not only enabled the creation of income, but also boosted the amount of the profit, and Section 1245 property, which enables the creation of income, but usually wears out and is actually used up over time, and does not go up in value.

If we analyze the Adams situation, we see that the package he sold consisted of $180,000 Duplex, $20,000 of land, $30,000 capital improvements, and $20,000 furniture and fixtures. The total is $250,000.

Adams is offered $400,000 for the Duplex and so we assume that this is the fair market value. That means that the property has increased in value by $150,000 which is an increase of 60%.

But let's look at it again. That $20,000 of furniture and fixtures is certainly not worth $32,000, which would mean that it increased in value 60% like all of the other elements of the package. It is probably worth close to the depreciated basis of $4,800 because it is in the process of wearing out.

However, if Adams does not separately identify the Section 1250 property and the Section 1245 property, and assign values to each item, he will be faced with depreciation recapture on the furniture and fixtures of $15,200 at his marginal tax rate of 39.6% because he used accelerated depreciation on it.

Therefore, he should assign a value to the furniture and fixtures of $4,800 and hope that this is not one of the 1031 Exchanges that the IRS looks at in a Random Audit. They will probably challenge it.

A better way to handle it would be to do a separate Bill of Sale prior to the closing from Adams to Baker for the furniture and fixtures for $4,800 and then subtract that from the $400,000 at closing, as I have suggested in the following Chapter on Personal Property.

Chapter 10

PERSONAL PROPERTY

OVERVIEW

"Personal property" does not mean your hair dryer or your fishing gear.

The IRS divides personal property into two types:

* depreciable personal property, and
* non-depreciable personal property.

"Depreciable" means that the property is used in a trade or business, and a depreciation allowance can be claimed as a deduction from income. The same property, not used in a trade or business, would not be "depreciable," so it would be non-depreciable personal property.

So, in classifying personal property, it does not depend on what it is, but depends on how it is used.

"Depreciable tangible personal property" means:

1.) it is personal property, not real property, and

2.) it is depreciable because it is being used in a trade or business and therefore you are allowed to deduct a depreciation amount as an expense over a period of time.

Generally, it means property that is business property, but it is not real estate.

There is a third category in addition to real property and depreciable personal property. It is called "other personal property."

"Other personal property" must be "held for investment" and includes art works, coin collections, antiques, copyrights, and patents. These items are like kind to each other, but only if they are very similar. For instance, a book copyright is not like kind to a song copyright.

As you can see, there is much uncertainty in this last area. In the area of personal property, "like kind" almost always means "identical."

ASSET CLASS

The IRS has identified 13 general classes of personal property assets.

00.11   Office furniture, fixtures, and equipment.

00.12   Information systems, i.e. computers and peripheral equipment.

00.13   Data handling equipment other than computers.

00.21   Airplanes and helicopters, including airframes and engines, except those used in commercial or contract carrying of passengers or freight.

00.22   Automobiles and taxis.

00.23   Passenger-carrying buses.

00.241   Light general purpose trucks.

00.242   Heavy general purpose trucks.

00.25   Railroad cars and locomotives, except those owned by railroad transportation companies.

00.26   Tractor units for use over-the-road.

00.27   Trailers, and trailer-mounted containers.

00.28   Vessels, barges, tugs, and similar water transportation equipment, except those used in marine construction.

00.29   Industrial steam and electric generation and/or distribution systems.

Assets in each class are like kind to assets in the same class.

Assets in one class are not like kind to assets in another class.

You will generally be replacing washers and dryers with washers and dryers, or refrigerators with refrigerators, etc., but if you find yourself in need of more detailed information, you can review Internal Revenue Bulletin 2004-38 entitled "Additional Rules for Exchanges of Personal Property Under Section 1031(a)." It is available at irs.gov/irb/2004-38_IRB/ar06.html.

ALWAYS IDENTIFY

There will be some Exchanges in which there is very little personal property involved.

For example, two washers and dryers valued at $500 included in the sale of a $400,000 Duplex.

The IRS will not disallow your Exchange is you fail to list the personal property separately, and just include the value with the price of the Duplex, and not try to match it with like kind personal property acquired as Replacement Property.

In fact, the practice has become that the IRS will allow the inclusion of personal property worth up to 15% of the fair market value of the combined real and personal property to be included without identification.

This means that if your $400,000 Duplex was actually $340,000 of Duplex and $60,000 of personal property (15% of $400,000), you would be permitted to ignore the $60,000 worth of personal property and treat it all as real property valued at $400,000.

But this is not a good idea for two reasons.

1.) The first reason is simply that the Exchange should be done correctly. You have probably been taking Accelerated Depreciation (probably Double Declining Balance) on the personal property and you need to document this fact and not just lump it in with straight-line depreciation. Later, if you sold the Duplex and you were paying tax on the recovery of this depreciation at 25% straight-line instead of 39.6% accelerated, you would be violating the law. This is a hook that the IRS could hang you on if they were ever so inclined.

2.) The second reason is even better. If you sell the $340,000 structure and the $60,000 worth of personal property and lump it together (remember, this is a simplified scenario used for the purpose of illustrating a point), and then replace it with a $650,000 structure and $100,000 worth of personal property and lump it together as $750,000 worth of real property, you will be leaving a lot of money on the table.

Here's why.

If you fail to separate out the $100,000 of new personal property, you will be depreciating it like it was real property, over a 27.5 year period.

Your annual depreciation allowance will be about $3,636.

But if you identify it and depreciate as "furniture and fixtures - rental" over a five year period, your depreciation allowance would be $20,000 per year.

And if the personal property were new, you would be allowed a Section 179 Bonus Depreciation for the first year of $50,000 and then regular depreciation the first year of up to $14,000 depending on which month it was placed in service.

In just the first year you would be shielding $64,000 in income and if you are in the 39.6% tax bracket, this is an extra $25,344 in your pocket.

You should always identify your personal property in your investment, and do the correct depreciation.

ALWAYS SELL IT SEPARATELY

As you recall, I explained the concept of Depreciation in Chapter 9. It is the periodic expensing of the purchase price of your asset over its life, while the asset is being used to earn income for you.

If you buy a $10,000 asset which is expected to last ten years, the IRS will allow you to deduct $1,000 of depreciation allowance from your yearly income. The assumption is that after ten years the asset will have no value and you will have received the benefit of deducting what you paid for it by reducing the taxable portion of your income $1,000 each year. You still received that extra $1,000 of income, you just didn't have to pay taxes on it. It was a periodic return of your investment.

And usually this assumption that you will use up all of the asset over time is true. If you operate a laundromat, you will be replacing the washers at just about the time you have fully depreciated them. They will have been used up and they will have no trade-in value.

But, if you have an apartment building which is furnished, you might have paid $500,000 for it, and assigned $50,000 to the value of the land, $400,000 to the value of the building, and

$50,000 to the value of the furnishings.

Now you have an offer of $1,000,000 for it after holding it for eight years.

That means that the value of everything has doubled.

Except that it hasn't!

The value of the land has probably at least doubled.

The value of the apartment building has probably doubled.

But the true market value of the furnishings is actually only what you could get for them at a garage sale, which is probably almost nothing. So, that $50,000 has not doubled, it has become zero.

But if you don't identify and separate out and sell the furnishings separately, they will be presumed to be worth $100,000 because you have been offered twice as much as you paid for the entire property. You will have depreciated them to zero, so you will have to recapture all of the $50,000 in accelerated depreciation, and with $1,000,000 in income, more than half of it being capital gains, putting you in the top marginal tax bracket, you will pay 39.6% tax on the depreciation recapture, which is $19,800.

But you can avoid this by doing a separate Bill of Sale for the furnishings for, say, $4,000 and assign the rest of the $1,000,000 sales price to the building and land. Your recapture tax will be $1,584 instead of $19,800, which is a savings of $18,216.

The $46,000 that you shifted to the real estate where it belongs could be assigned $16,000 to the land and $30,000 to the building. It will be taxed at the 20% capital gains rate, which is $9,200. Subtract this from your savings of $18,216 and you end up with a net savings of $9,016. Not bad for just a little bookkeeping.

Understanding and using depreciation correctly can make the difference between being a successful investor and a very successful investor.

Chapter 11

VACATION HOME

QUALIFICATION

A so-called "vacation home" is really just a second personal residence. It doesn't take on a new identity because you stay in it while you are on vacation, or wearing shorts, or away from your primary residence for the weekend.

Even if you do not stay in it, and you only bought it for investment, the IRS does not consider it qualified for treatment as an investment under the Section 1031 requirement of "property held for productive use in a trade or business or held for investment."

A second home or vacation home will not qualify for Relinquished Property in a Section 1031 Like Kind Exchange if it is currently used exclusively for personal use, regardless of how long you have owned it.

A second home or vacation home will not qualify for Replacement Property in a 1031 Exchange if you plan to use it exclusively for personal use after you acquire it.

However, it can qualify for both Relinquished Property and Replacement Property if it is also used for rental income as well as personal use.

The rule for a vacation home is that it must be listed for rental, usually with a property manager or by running ads in the newspaper, and your personal use must not exceed 14 days, or 10% of the actual number of days rented, whichever number is greater.

So, if you use the property for personal use one week out of the year, you must rent it out for at least ten weeks. That satisfies the 10% requirement. If you use the property two weeks each year, the maximum allowed, you must rent it out for at least twenty weeks. That satisfies both the 10% requirement and the 14 day requirement.

Otherwise, it does not qualify as Relinquished Property for Section 1031 treatment if you sell it.

Also, if you buy it as Replacement Property, the same rules apply, and the IRS is very strict about this.

During the time that you own the vacation home, the rental income and details of your personal use of the home, are reported on Schedule E, which is attached to your Form 1040.

If you plan to qualify the property as Relinquished Property, you probably should be able to show, through rental income records, how the property was used for two years prior to the Exchange.

If you plan to qualify the property as Replacement Property, you should begin immediately after purchase to qualify and continue through the remainder of the tax year and another full tax year to avoid any question.

Since this is a frequent source of conflict with taxpayers, the IRS has provided Internal Revenue Bulletin 2008-16, which is a Safe Harbor for such transactions. It is actually one of the better-written bulletins, and will probably be understandable to a layman. You can find it at irs.gov/irb/2008-16_IRB/.

IRB 2008-16 says that the IRS will not question whether a dwelling unit was held for use in a trade or business if the taxpayer has owned the Relinquished Property for at least 24 months prior to the Exchange Date (not two tax years, but 24 consecutive months), and rented it for at least 14 days each of those two 12-months periods, and has not personally used it for more than 14 days, or 10% of the total number of days rented, whichever is greater, for each of those two 12-month periods. For Replacement Property, the same rules apply. Do this, and the IRS will not challenge the use qualification.

Remember to check for free updates at:
www.S1031Exchange.com

You will also find expanded articles on all aspects of Section 1031 Like Kind Exchanges, and articles on related subjects like Deductions, Depreciation, Repairs, and Tax Accounting.

Chapter 12

121 PERSONAL RESIDENCE RULE

NO CAPITAL GAINS TAX

Of all the assets that you own, there is one asset that you can sell without having to pay taxes on your profit.

IRS Section 121 covers the sale of a residence occupied by the taxpayer for at least two of the five years prior to sale.

A single taxpayer can exclude $250,000 of gain from such a sale.

A married taxpayer can exclude $500,000 of gain. The husband and wife must have both lived in the house for the two qualifying years, and they must file a joint tax return. The house can be in the name of either one of them, or in the names of both.

This does not mean that you must own the house for five years. It means that you have a five-year period in which to accumulate the two years of occupancy. You can sell your personal residence every two years and avoid paying taxes on your capital gains.

Your occupancy of two years out of five years does not have to be continuous or consecutive. You can satisfy the two-year requirement in smaller increments. Or you can live in it for two years and rent it for three, or vice versa, and still sell it and claim the Section 121 exemption.

However, if you claimed depreciation during the rental period, you will have to recapture this depreciation amount at a 25% tax rate. You report it on Form 4797 and transfer that to Schedule D.

If you do decide to qualify your residency during a continuous two-year period, you may still have temporary and periodic absences for vacation or "seasonal" absences and keep the time period running.

The rules for Section 121 are fairly simple, and you can find more information in the IRS Publication 523 Selling Your Home. It is available at irs.gov/pub/irs-pdf/p523.pdf.

The next Chapter will show you how to use Section 121 in combination with Section 1031 to rack up some real tax savings.

Chapter 13

COMBINING SECTIONS 1031 AND 121

MIXED USE

Sometimes the transaction will involve a personal residence combined with other property that is business or investment property.

This is called "mixed use" and it involves applying the rules of both Section 121 and Section 1031.

For example, a 100-acre farm might contain the 95 acres of farm land, and then the house and 5 acres. The farm is the business that comes under Section 1031, and the house is the personal residence that comes under Section 121.

Also, a motel might contain the office, lounge, laundry, and rental units, and then contain a separate living unit which is the owner's residence. It doesn't even have to be physically separate, but capable of being dealt with separately as far as separating out the numbers.

If you are involved in such a transaction, you will want to allocate as much of the property as possible into the personal residence category and take advantage of the Section 121 exemption, because all of that capital gains could be tax-free.

Then you can do a Section 1031 Like Kind Exchange with the remainder of the property, and defer the tax on that capital gains by investing the net sales proceeds in a new investment property.

Sometimes you will actually want to plan ahead to create a situation where you can take advantage of the Section 121 Exemption as part of what would otherwise be a Section 1031 Exchange.

You can sell a Relinquished Property in which you have, say a $100,000 profit, and purchase a residential property as a Replacement Property and rent it out for one or two years to satisfy the "intent" requirement of Section 1031 that the property be "held for productive use in a trade or business" and then move into it as your personal residence. You have converted Section 1031 property into Section 121 property.

After living in the property for at least two years, on a date that is at least five years from the date on which the property was received in a Section 1031 Exchange, you can sell it and pay no capital gains tax from the first transaction or on any increase in profit, up to the limit of $500,000. However, you will have to pay the tax on the Depreciation Recapture from the first transaction, and you must recapture the depreciation taken while it was an investment property before you moved into it. But you can pocket the rest of the net sales proceeds.

You can also do this conversion in the other direction.

You might have a residence in which your profit would be $600,000 if you sold it under Section 121, and after claiming the $500,000 exemption you would still owe taxes on the remaining $100,000.

You can move out of the house and make it a rental property.

You should sign a contract with a management company and make sure that the house is advertised for rent. You move into another house. You change the address on your drivers license, credit cards, voter registration, and library card.

After at least one year, and preferably more, your property qualifies for a Section 1031 Exchange.

You can then sell it and claim a Section 121 Exemption for $500,000 of your profit because you have lived in it for two of the prior five years. You can use the other $100,000 of your profit to combine with a $400,000 bank loan and buy another $500,000 rental property and qualify for a Section 1031 Exchange.

You should always structure your transactions so that they look like a real business transaction, which they are, instead of looking like they have no purpose other than avoiding taxes. It is legal to avoid taxes, but you should do so while you are managing your investments in a business-like manner.

Author's Note:

I will be, in addition to constantly updating this book, working on new chapters to go into the next edition, tentatively scheduled for publication in January of 2019. If you have a suggestion for a subject to be covered, you can leave feedback at:

www.S1031Exchange.com

Chapter 14

CONCLUSION

Most of the attention today in the world of real estate involves flash and hustle for making quick profit. And there can be lots of money to be made. But the individuals doing this are always scrambling for the next deal, and are always living with the risk that they will lose money instead of making money.

The real estate professionals who end up with a large portfolio of properties and a life of luxury are focusing on the long term. Much of their property was bought with money available to them because they deferred taxes on their capital gains, and then borrowed four times that amount to put together the investment funds. They are viewed by lenders as good business managers.

Most of the remainder of their property was bought with borrowed funds. When an investment property went up 20% in value over a three or four year period of time, they enjoyed a 100% return on their out-of-pocket investment because they only put up the down payment.

They found good safe investments and converted them into other larger investments over time, and eventually became wealthy.

The key to their long term investment strategy involved using Section 1031 Like Kind Exchange and Section 121 Home Sale

Exemption in order to defer and avoid taxation of their profits, along with leverage and timing.

They could have easily started with an investment fund as small as $40,000 and turned it into investment property worth $30 Million within 30 years.

Eventually they passed their wealth to family members through inheritance without ever paying the deferred capital gains because the property passed to the family members with a new basis of the Fair Market Value, and when the family members sold it, at that Fair Market Value, they had no profit, and so no tax liability.

Understanding a fair amount of tax law, a little bit of finance, and a little bit of accounting can make you a very wealthy person.

And let me take this additional opportunity to warn you about choosing the wrong Qualified Intermediary, or turning this over to a real estate salesperson. Look at the YouTube videos viewed by tens of thousands of people and see where these self-described experts are actually saying that you must deed your property to the Qualified Intermediary who will then sell it to the Buyer, or that "like kind" just means that both properties are real estate. This borders on ignorance. Please be careful.

I hope you have gained some benefit from this book, and that you will go to S1031Exchange.com and sign up for notification of the Updates, so that the book will remain new for you until the next Edition.

And please visit me at www.MichaelLantrip.com.

Thank you.

APPENDIX A - INCOME TAX RATES

Taxpayers with different levels of income pay different amounts of tax.

But they also pay a different percentage of their income in taxes.

This is because we have a graduated system of taxation.

The different levels of taxation are called "marginal tax brackets."

The numbers will be different for a single person, but in my example here, I will use the numbers for a married couple who are filing a joint tax return.

For each dollar of Taxable Income that you have, starting with the first dollar, and going up to and including $18,450 you will pay taxes at the rate of 10% of your income.

But when dollar number 18,451 is added to your Taxable Income total, you will be taxed at 15% on that dollar, and on each dollar after that up to and including dollar number 74,900. In other words, you have moved from the 10% tax bracket into the 15% tax bracket, and, as you can see, each of these new tax brackets is a "marginal tax bracket."

With each dollar of Taxable Income in the $74,901 marginal tax bracket you will be taxed at the rate of 25% and you will stay in this marginal tax bracket through dollar number 151,200.

The next marginal tax bracket is 28% and it starts at $151,201.

The 33% marginal tax bracket starts at $230,451.

The 35% marginal tax bracket starts at $411,501.

And the highest tax bracket, 39.6%, starts at $464,851.

What this all means is that each dollar of your Total Taxable Income that you earn in each of these brackets will be taxed at a different rate.

BUT, your Taxable Income is not your total income. That's why the term "Taxable Income" is capitalized, to signify that it is a computed number created with a formula, and not just the total of everything that you receive.

The best way to understand this is to look at your own tax return, Form 1040.

Lines 7 through 21 are your individual items of Income, which are totaled on line 22 and called total income. But, as I said, this is not your Taxable Income.

Then on lines 23 through 35 you are allowed to claim "adjustments" to your income, like alimony paid, IRA deductions, tuition, and so forth. These are totaled on line 36 and subtracted from your total income on line 22. The result on line 37 is called your adjusted gross income, referred to as AGI. This is still not your Taxable Income.

From this you subtract your $12,400 Standard Itemized Deduction allowance and your $7,900 Exemptions amount, and, finally, you will arrive at your Taxable Income.

You will find it on line 43.

This is the number that you need to know.

Let's compute the tax on that. Say the number on line 43 is $75,000 and all of it is ordinary income, such as W2, and none of it is capital gains or stock dividends.

The first $18,450 will be taxed at 10%, resulting in $1,845.00 in taxes.

The next amount, $56,450 (74,900 minus 18,450) will be taxed at 15%, resulting in $8,467.50 in taxes.

The next amount, $100 (75,000 minus 74,900) will be taxed at 25%, resulting in $25.00 in taxes.

Your total tax liability will be $10,337.50 (1,845.00 plus 8,467.50 plus 25.00).

This is 13.78% of your taxable income of $75,000.

So, even though you are in the 25% marginal tax bracket, your "effective tax rate," the percentage of your Taxable Income that you pay in taxes, is only 13.78%.

Marginal tax rates and effective tax rates are very important factors in making business and investment decisions, and you should understand them.

You can view all of the Tax Tables, and even work through examples, at irs.gov/pub/irs-pdf/i1040tt.pdf.

APPENDIX B - CAPITAL GAINS TAX RATES

If you have worked through the examples of the four Section 1031 Like Kind Exchanges with me, you have a basic understanding of what long term capital gains are, and how they are taxed at the top rate of 20%. Remember, short term capital gains are taxed at your ordinary marginal tax rate.

In recent years, the rules regarding long term capital gains have become very complicated, with different rates for different people, and the rules have more to do with the social status of the taxpayer than with the business transaction itself. Two investors, each making $70,000 profit from selling a real estate investment, will each have a different amount of taxes taken from them by the government, depending on who they are. One might have nothing taken and the other one might have 20% taken.

If you search the irs.gov website for information you will be sent to irs.gov/pub/irs-pdf/i1040tt.pdf. But this does not contain the capital gains tax tables, just the ordinary income tax tables, which were referenced previously in Appendix A.

Apparently, the IRS has chosen not to create a Capital Gains Tax Table, nor a Publication explaining the subject.

But here is a recap of the Ordinary Income Tax Rates, with the Capital Gains Tax Rate added. This is for Married, Filing Jointly.

* If your Taxable Income is from $0 - $18,450 your Income Tax Rate is 10% and your Capital Gains Tax Rate is 0%.

* If your Taxable Income is $18,451 - $74,900 your marginal Income Tax Rate is 15% and your Capital Gains Tax Rate is 0%.

* If your Taxable Income is $74,901 - $151,200 your marginal Income Tax Rate is 25% and your Capital Gains Tax Rate is 15%.

* If your Taxable Income is $151,201 - $230,450 your marginal Income Tax Rate is 28% and your Capital Gains Tax Rate is 15%.

* If your Taxable Income is $230,451 - $411,500 your marginal Income Tax Rate is 33% and your Capital Gains Tax Rate is 15%.

* If your Taxable Income is $411,501 - $464,850 your marginal Income Tax Rate is 35% and your Capital Gains Tax Rate is 15%.

* If your Taxable Income is $464,851 or more, your marginal Income Tax Rate is 39.6% and your Capital Gains Tax Rate is 20%.

However, if your capital gains results from the sale of what is called "qualified small business stock" or from selling collectibles, like coins or art, the maximum Capital Gains Tax Rate is 28%.

If you would like to work through a computation on your anticipated capital gains, you can find a worksheet on the last two pages of the Instructions for Schedule D, which is located at irs.gov/pub/irs-pdf/i1040sd.pdf.

APPENDIX C - TEXT OF IRC SECTION 1031

Instead of posting the text of Section 1031, I will connect you to the source that I use for all of my references. It is the Legal Information Institute (LII) website operated by Cornell University Law School.

The complete text of Section 1031 can be found at: www.law.cornell.edu/uscode/text/26/1031

Also, if you click on the "Notes" tab, you can read all of the Amendments to Section 1031 going back to 1958.

And one of my favorite places to go on the entire web is found behind the "IRS Rulings" tab.

This list is updated daily by LII and apparently every Friday by the IRS.

Here you will find all of the "Written Determinations by the IRS regarding Section 1031." These are sometimes referred to as "Private Letter Rulings."

If you click on a Private Letter Ruling you will get a printable PDF of the actual letter sent by the IRS to the taxpayer who requested the ruling.

These Private Letter Rulings are usually about twelve pages long and involve a complicated set of facts.

They are not likely to match your situation exactly, or even closely, but among the discussions of various issues you might find explanations that will clarify points that you are having trouble with.

At S1031Exchange.com, I will be alerting you to any new postings, with an explanation of what they are, and which chapter in this book is affected by them.

APPENDIX D - TEXT OF REG. SEC. 1.1031

The text for Regulation 1.1031 is very extensive and the easiest way to deal with it is to go to the Legal Information Institute (LII) website operated by Cornell University Law School. It is better than anything I could provide here. It's what I use.

Start with the Table of Contents of Reg. 1.1031 available here: www.law.cornell.edu/cfr/text/26/1.1031-0

Find the paragraph or subsection that you want by reading the headings and clicking on one. You will be taken to the full text of the law.

If you click on the "Rulemaking" tab, you can see all of the rules, proposed rules, and notices published in the Federal Register about the paragraph you are viewing.

This is the most extensive package of information available anywhere, and we are all deeply indebted to Cornell University Law School.